APPROACHES TO THE
AMERICAN MUSICAL

EXETER STUDIES IN
AMERICAN AND COMMONWEALTH ARTS
GENERAL EDITOR: RICHARD MALTBY

APPROACHES TO THE AMERICAN MUSICAL is a volume in Exeter
Studies in American and Commonwealth Arts, a series produced by
AmCAS, the Centre for American and Commonwealth Arts in the
University of Exeter. Other volumes in the series include AMERICAN
CULTURAL CRITICS, edited by David Murray; REPRESENTING
OTHERS: White views of Indigenous Peoples, edited by Mick Gidley;
LOCATING THE SHAKERS: Cultural Origins and Legacies of an
American Religious Movement, edited by Mick Gidley with Kate Bowles.

APPROACHES TO THE
AMERICAN MUSICAL

Edited by
Robert Lawson-Peebles

UNIVERSITY
of
EXETER
PRESS

First published in 1996 by
University of Exeter Press
Reed Hall, Streatham Drive
Exeter, Devon EX4 4QR
UK

British Library Cataloguing in Publication Data
A catalogue record of this book is available
from the British Library

ISBN 0 85989 405 3

Typeset in Walbaum
by GreenShires Icon, Exeter

Printed and bound in Great Britain
by BPC Wheatons Ltd, Exeter

Contents

Copyright Acknowledgements

Notes on Contributors

Stephen Banfield is Elgar Professor of Music and Head of Performance Studies at the University of Birmingham, England. He is the author of *Sensibility and English Song* and *Sondheim's Broadway Musicals,* and editor of the twentieth-century volume of *The Blackwell History of Music in Britain.*

Ann-Charlotte Hanes Harvey is a dramaturg, translator and performer, and is Professor of Drama at San Diego State University, California, USA.

David Horn is Director of the Institute of Popular Music, University of Liverpool, England. He is co-ordinating editor of the journal *Popular Music.*

Robert Lawson-Peebles is Senior Lecturer in the School of English and American Studies, University of Exeter, England. He is the author of *Landscape and Written Expression in Revolutionary America* and co-editor of *Views of American Landscapes* and *Modern American Landscapes.*

Wilfrid Mellers is Professor of Music Emeritus at the University of York, England. Among his many books are *Music in a New Found Land: Themes and developments in the history of American music* and *Twilight of the Gods: The Beatles in Retrospect.*

Sue Rickard was, amongst other things, a classical guitar teacher before taking a BA and MA at Exeter University. She now teaches for the Open University, England.

Carey Wall is Professor of English at San Diego State University, California, USA. She has published on William Faulkner, Mark Twain and Eudora Welty.

Ralph Willett recently retired as Senior Lecturer in the Department of American Studies, University of Hull, England. His publications include *The Open Cage: American Film 1935–60* and *The Americanization of Germany.*

1

Introduction: Cultural Musicology and the American Musical

Robert Lawson-Peebles

As its size perhaps indicates, this book is not another picture-laden homage to the American musical. It is, rather, an attempt to give serious (but not solemn) attention to aspects of a genre which can claim a long pedigree but whose modern form is just under seventy years old.

The origins of the musical can be traced back to the amalgamation of dramatic structure and popular song in John Gay's *The Beggar's Opera*, first produced in 1728 and popular in America in the 1740s.[1] As its name suggests, *The Beggar's Opera* united elements drawn from opposite ends of the social spectrum. The American musical has been similarly, and possibly just as deliberately, indiscriminate. It draws on vaudeville and the so-called "legitimate" theatre, on burlesque and opera. It is in a direct line of descent, on the one hand, from Gilbert and Sullivan, French *opéra bouffe* and German operetta; and on the other from the rich tradition of indigenous popular song which dates at least back to Francis Hopkinson (1737–91), a signatory to the Declaration of Independence and credited as the first American songwriter.[2] In the view of most critics, *Show Boat* (1927), by Jerome Kern and Oscar Hammerstein II, is the first mature musical.[3] In the following forty years the musical enjoyed a period of great popularity, enhanced by Hollywood and embracing such figures as Kern, the Gershwin brothers,

1

Rodgers and Hart (and then Rodgers and Hammerstein), Irving Berlin and Cole Porter, Lerner and Loewe, Kander and Ebb, Frank Loesser and Leonard Bernstein. Its demise has frequently been forecast in the last twenty years or so, but it still survives in the work of Stephen Sondheim.[4]

There are a number of good reasons why *Show Boat* is a benchmark in the history of the musical. Firstly, it handles an array of contemporary social concerns such as miscegenation, gambling, alcoholism and failed marriages. Second, it deploys a range of popular song to answer the demands of a structured, if convoluted, plot. For instance, one song, "You Are Love," looks appropriately, if ironically, back to operetta. This European form was imported into the New World by the Bohemian Rudolf Friml, whose first successful American operetta was *The Firefly* (1912); by the Hungarian Sigmund Romberg, best known for *The Student Prince* (1924) and *The Desert Song* (1926); and Victor Herbert, who left Dublin at the age of three, receiving his musical training in Stuttgart before emigrating to the United States to achieve fame as the composer of *Mlle. Modiste* (1904) and *Naughty Marietta* (1910). Another song in *Show Boat*, "Can't Help Lovin' Dat Man," invokes another tradition by attempting to synthesize white and Black American indigenous music. Kern was by no means the first songwriter to do this. The Irish-American Stephen Foster (1826–64) was trained by a German musician in Pittsburgh, began his career as a composer by writing a waltz, but made his name with such "Ethiopian Melodies" as "Oh! Susanna" and "Camptown Races," stereotyped yet sympathetic approaches to Black song. Similarly, George Gershwin's first big hit was "Swanee" (1920), performed in blackface by Al Jolson.

In contrast, music *performed* by Black people, as opposed to music *about* or *influenced* by Black people, had a much more limited reception. Until the changes wrought by the Civil Rights movement of the 1950s and 60s, few Black musicals had a widespread audience. *In Dahomey* (1903) was the first Black show to have a regular Broadway run. It starred the dancers Bert Williams and George Walker, and led to the enormous, if brief, popularity of the Cakewalk. *Shuffle Along* (1921), written by Noble Sissle and Eubie Blake, and including the song "I'm Just

2

Wild About Harry," surmounted financial shortages and racial prejudice to run for 504 performances. In contrast, *Treemonisha* (1911), Scott Joplin's ambitious attempt to fuse Ragtime and opera, received only one performance in Joplin's lifetime, and did not see the light of day again until the Ragtime revival, assisted by the film *The Sting* (1973), prompted musicologist Günther Schuller to orchestrate Joplin's piano score, leading to productions in Houston and New York. In vernacular music as in many other spheres of life, white practice (intentionally or not) tended to dispossess Black. Indeed, the nearest thing to a popular Black protest song for some years was "Ol' Man River," regarded by many as the most serious moment in *Show Boat*.[5]

One climactic moment of *Show Boat*, set in Chicago at New Year's Eve 1904, is endowed with a sense of its period by the inclusion of four songs written by other composers popular in the preceding twenty years. Amongst them is Charles K. Harris's "After the Ball," the first song to sell a million copies. By the turn of the century, songwriting had become a big industry, focussed particularly on 28th Street in Manhattan, where the noise of assembled songpluggers battering pianos to the latest melodies gave the street the name Tin Pan Alley. The industry catered to a growing range of demands as immigration expanded (bringing amongst others Friml, Romberg and Herbert to the United States) in the years before the Quota Act of 1921 introduced restrictions. Irving Berlin, for instance, wrote Yiddish songs reflecting his childhood as well as Irish ballads, Italian love songs, and such affectionate looks at contemporary Black culture as "Alexander's Ragtime Band" (1911). One of the factors unifying such songs is that they came from or concerned oppressed minority groups. Isaac Goldberg, a Harvard professor who was the friend and first biographer of George Gershwin, speculated in 1930 that such groups provided the "American Anglo-Saxon" with examples of what he called the "foreigner" (and what we would call "the other"), "credited with a fine intensity of inner life and with passions less bridled than those of the more conventional."[6] Indeed, it could be said that one of the strengths of *Show Boat* is that it captures a fine, if flawed, intensity of inner life.

This sketch of the context of *Show Boat* says something, I

hope, about the variety and vitality of this form of American popular culture. Why, then, hasn't it received more sustained and serious attention? The answer, I think, concerns the status of the musical. In its time, *The Beggar's Opera* was controversial. Likewise, the status of its modern American counterpart has never been certain. An account of "musical comedy," for instance, did not appear in *Grove's Dictionary of Music and Musicians* until the *New Grove* of 1980.[7] It has had a chequered critical history, for a number of reasons. I have already hinted at one of them. The musical has too often been subjected to breathless adulation. Here is one of the less purple examples, from a book which otherwise has some sensible points to make about the genre:

> ...ultimately, the Broadway musical is a metaphor for the ecstasy we are capable of creating and experiencing; it offers us an emotional orgasm. The Broadway musical is not a passive theater. Its audiences are transformed as they are being made love to. They sing and dance as they make their way up the aisles while the walkout music is being played. They are not out of the theater yet. The music goes on, and as it goes on they take the show with them. Not yet out of the theater, they are still wearing the show on their faces. On the sidewalk they are different from the other people. They're fresh from peaking, not quite back to the real life.
>
> Well, it was only a show: music, lyrics, libretto, costumes, lighting, actors, dancers. Yet something bigger had been made, something liberating. This has been no drama, not a comedy. Theater, yes, but a special kind of theater with only one fit name for it: the Broadway musical.[8]

The prose here itself employs an extended sexual metaphor as a vehicle to make special claims for the genre, diverting the reader from realizing that the effect created in the audience is by no means an ability of the musical alone. Many cinemagoers have felt precisely the same effect, perhaps even intensified by the greater darkness needed for films. Both audiences, moreover, are experiencing a modern version of catharsis, the rhetoric of tragedy described in Aristotle's *Poetics*.[9] The Broadway musical, then, is by no means "a special kind of theater" in this respect, and this claim for it invites ridicule.

Many critics have taken a much darker view of the musical, deriding it as more than ridiculous, indeed as positively evil. They have taken their cue from Amanda Prynne who, in Noel Coward's 1930 play *Private Lives*, remarks that it is "extraordinary how potent cheap music is." Coward's work was frequently noted for its blend of badinage and asperity, but the cutting edge of this remark may have been honed by his awareness of competition from American musicals, which were transferring with increasing success to London's West End stage. For instance, both *Show Boat* and the Gershwins' *Funny Face* (with Fred and Adèle Astaire) opened with great success in London within twelve months of their 1927 Broadway premières.[10] I am speculating. What is not speculative is that potency and cheapness quickly became common images in the negative critical vocabulary of the musical.

With some reason (as we shall see later) the musical has often been associated with the capitalist market system; with much less reason, it is supposed to be a mass-produced form. For both reasons it has been used as a political football, regarded as nothing more than a debased, commercial vehicle of pseudo feelings. The American art critic Clement Greenberg, for instance, listed "Tin Pan Alley music" and tap-dancing, two important components of the musical, as among the many modern phenomena that were "Kitsch." Another American, the political and social critic Dwight MacDonald, came to the same conclusion. He coined the term "Masscult," contrasting it with "Folk Art," which, he thought, was a genuine art-expression of ordinary people. MacDonald singled out Jazz as a Folk Art, having both an intellectual content and a popular appeal. In contrast Masscult, he believed, was an imposition from above, "fabricated by technicians hired by businessmen"; and he added, with typical acerbity: "It is not just unsuccessful art. It is non-art. It is even anti-art." MacDonald also coined the term "midcult," in his view a saccharine corruption of "high culture" for the middlebrow American audience. Examples of midcult were "the folk-fakery of *Oklahoma!* and the orotund sentimentalities of *South Pacific*."[11]

Across the Atlantic there were many critics, of various nationalities and political persuasions, who agreed with the point of

5

view held by Greenberg and MacDonald, and they added the animus which has frequently soured Old World attitudes to the New. Continental criticism tended to be the more politically systematic. Many continental critics agreed with the German Marxist Theodor Adorno, who saw the musical as part of a "culture industry" which deceived the working class, replacing genuine inspiration with a standardized and stylized "barbarity."

British criticism tended to be less politically oriented. Instead, it followed the aesthetic and moral commentary of Matthew Arnold, who in 1869 had defined culture as the "disinterested pursuit of perfection," and in 1888 had complained that American civilization was not "interesting" because it lacked "elevation and beauty." Traces of Arnold's critique may be found in the work of writers as various as the popular philosopher C. E. M. Joad, the literary critic F. R. Leavis, the novelist George Orwell and the journalist Francis Williams.[12] Their definition of culture is less restricted than his, but their work is more shrill due to their awareness of the growing influence of American popular idioms, which in their view resembled insidious organisms undermining and driving out indigenous and apparently more "natural" forms of expression. A latter-day example of this belief is to be found in *The Uses of Literacy* (1957), the influential jeremiad by the critic Richard Hoggart, which talks darkly of "aesthetic breakdown" and cites the "nickelodeon" and the "five-million-dollar film" as examples of "a peculiarly thin and pallid form of dissipation, a sort of spiritual dry-rot." There seems to be a contemptuous energy informing the hyphenation of that production cost. Hoggart was writing at a time of renewed popularity of Hollywood films with British cinema audiences, in part because of the use of such expensive techniques as Technicolor and Cinemascope. It must be said, though, that only a few films in the 1950s cost as much as five million dollars. Those that did tended to be biblical epics such as *The Robe* ($5M) or musicals such as *Guys and Dolls* ($5.5M, 1955) and *South Pacific* ($5M, 1958).[13]

Much critical disdain of the American musical is derived from the concept of aesthetic autonomy. The concept dates back to the Renaissance and is to be found, for instance, in Giorgio Vasari's *Lives of the Artists*. Vasari's desire to raise the status of

6

artists like Leonardo separated the arts from
humbler relation, the crafts, and developed int
they inhabited a superior realm, transcending th
and space. Of course, this argument is all the mo
tained with non-representational arts, like mai
music. It is for this reason that the literary and art ci
Pater claimed, in a book appropriately looking bac
Renaissance, that *"all art constantly aspires toward th* *..di-*
tion of music" and that at its best an art like poetry or painting
left behind such "mere matter" as "the actual circumstances of
an event, the actual topography of a landscape," becoming
"abstract" and "an end in itself." That was in 1873. Eighty years
later the concept of music as *the* non-representational form had
grown so strong that the philosopher Suzanne Langer could
claim that "music swallows words." In effect, words did not
matter. As Langer remarked, "trivial or sentimental lyrics may
be good texts as well as great poems."[14]

The concept of aesthetic autonomy had two consequences.
The first was that music irrevocably stained with the conditions
of its creation, like much pop and most musicals, was demoted
to a craft or, as we have seen, to the worse status of a produc-
tion-line object. Second, the idealist impulse of music took its
attendant analytical discipline, musicology, with it. It has
tended to exempt musicology from the debates which in the last
couple of decades changed first literary criticism and then art
criticism. As Richard Leppert and Susan McClary noted in 1987:

> For the most part, the discourse of musical scholarship clings
> stubbornly to a reliance on positivism in historical research
> and formalism in theory and criticism, with primary attention
> still focused almost exclusively on the canon.[15]

In consequence, many musicologists were singularly ill-
equipped, indeed unwilling, to analyze the musical.

A number of appropriate analytical instruments have existed
for some time. They are adapted from the social sciences, particularly anthropology and sociology, which employed a more
comprehensive definition of culture as a complex, multifaceted
organism involving a variety of interactive structures and hier-
archies.[16] Ironically, a number of critics have used the social

ience definition of culture to denigrate American popular idioms. For instance *Middletown*, described when it first appeared in 1929 as "a pioneer attempt to deal with a sample American community after the manner of social anthropology," was promptly quoted by F. R. Leavis in a pamphlet denouncing, amongst other things, Hollywood films.[17] In more recent years, however, anthropology has been used by cultural critics with greater rigor and in a way that is both more detailed and more contemplative. They have been influenced by the work of Claude Lévi-Strauss and Clifford Geertz. Lévi-Strauss has shown that cultures are characterized by great variety but united by deep structures analogous to a language. The task of the cultural critic, therefore, is to record the individual components of a culture and to show their place in its structure. Geertz, who is both an admirer and a critic of Lévi-Strauss, has suggested that culture is something that is created in the process of observation, and is not an objective structure to be observed by the detached analyst. As Geertz eloquently remarked in a 1973 essay:

> Believing ... that man is an animal suspended in webs of significance he himself has spun, I take culture to be those webs, and the analysis of it to be therefore not an experimental science in search of law but an interpretive one in search of meaning ... culture is not a power, something to which social events, behaviors, institutions, or processes can be causally attributed; it is a context, something within which they can be intelligibly—that is, thickly—described.[18]

A "thick description" of Leavis's use of *Middletown* would not focus on Hollywood films as a threat, but instead would look at Leavis's reasons for perceiving them as a threat. Such reasons might include, at increasing levels of specificity, transatlantic relations of the time, contemporary attitudes to connections between film and literature, changes in British industrial methods, Leavis's sense of "Englishness," his perceptions of the place of Cambridge University (his lifelong intellectual if often uncomfortable "home") in the defense of "Englishness," and the films being shown at local cinemas while he was writing about *Middletown*. A thicker description would include my own reasons for using the example of Leavis and *Middletown*.

Obviously, "thick description" is complex and time-consuming, and many of its components may be irrecoverable. The work of Lévi-Strauss has had a greater influence on literary and cultural criticism than that of Geertz. Neither has yet had much impact on musicology, with the sole exception—for obvious reasons—of ethnomusicology.[19] To date, musicologists have drawn more extensively on cultural critics whose work has a political rather than an anthropological content.[20] The strongest impact has been made by Theodor Adorno. While Adorno disliked popular music, his insistence that one must attend to the conditions of production and its consequences on musical form at least recognized the possibility of a sophisticated sociohistorical analysis of the genre. His influence has been acknowledged by, among others, Richard Middleton writing on popular music, as well as Susan McClary on Bach and Alastair Williams on Ligeti.[21] The work of the Italian Marxist philosopher Antonio Gramsci has also been influential. Gramsci wrote in the 1920s and 1930s about the concept of "hegemony," a term denoting the covert ways in which a dominated (or "subaltern") class is persuaded to embrace the ideology of the dominant class. His work became well known after the publication of selections in English in 1971, and it had a strong influence on, for example, the work of Dick Hebdige on such subcultures as reggae and punk rock.[22] More recently, the work of the Russian literary critic Mikhail Bakhtin has helped to explain why hegemonic structures are never fully successful. Through his studies on the novel, Bakhtin suggested that language, because it is discourse, is essentially "dialogical" (that is, pluralistic), will not allow itself to be confined to a specific meaning. Certain modes of discourse are, to use his term, "carnivalesque"; that is, they contain an assault on the dominant ideology, a reversal of social norms. Michael Holquist sums up Bakhtin's work, and also confirms, in a different context, the remarks by Clifford Geertz, quoted earlier, when he asserts that:

> There is no such thing as a "general language," a language
> that is spoken by a general voice, that may be divorced from
> a specific saying, which is charged with particular overtones.

9

> Language, when it *means*, is somebody talking to somebody
> else, even when that someone else is one's own inner
> addressee.

Bakhtin's work has had a significant influence on literary and cultural studies, and is having a growing impact on musicology.[23]

The present volume is an attempt to develop the project that Joseph Kerman has called "cultural musicology."[24] It tries to find common ground by bringing together American Studies specialists and musicologists.

It is for me a particular pleasure to include in the volume two essays by Wilfrid Mellers, who is unusual amongst senior British musicologists not only in his breadth of interests but also in his sensitivity to the environment in which music is created.[25] In his first contribution, Mellers sets the temporal and geographical bounds of this volume by relating the use of "Nessun Dorma" as the theme-music for the 1990 World Cup broadcasts on BBCTV—and the consequent appearance in the pop charts of the recording by Luciano Pavarotti—to the first production, in 1904, of *Madama Butterfly*. The discussion of Puccini is a particularly appropriate starting-point for a book on the musical, for several reasons. The intense, almost cloying sweetness of Puccini's melodies may be discerned in a number of musicals. Secondly, Puccini problematizes the jolly orientalism to be found in Gilbert and Sullivan's *The Mikado* (1885) and transforms his work into an American opera by means of his account of cross-cultural sexual relationships. Between 1880 and 1930 twenty-seven million people migrated to America, many of them from cultures regarded as "alien" by older-established Americans. As a result, questions of ethnicity, identity and cultural imperialism—the whole "melting-pot" syndrome—became a focus of debate that has never been satisfactorily resolved, as has been more recently shown by *Pacific Overtures* (1976), Stephen Sondheim's acid contribution to the American Bicentennial celebrations.[26] Third, in both *Madama Butterfly* and *La Fanciulla del West* (*The Girl of the Golden West*, 1910), Puccini darkened the romantic melodramas of the

10

American playwright and actor-manager, David Belasco, in consequence highlighting the conflict between the Old World and the New and interrogating some central American myths. The American sailor who abandons Cio-Cio-San is deliberately given the name of Benjamin Franklin Pinkerton. Benjamin Franklin (1706–90), perhaps now better known as America's leading eighteenth-century scientist and philosopher and the epitome of the ideology of self-help, was also noted for his winning ways with French ladies. Allan Pinkerton (1819–94) created an espionage system during the Civil War, and later formed industrial police for strike-breaking. It is clear that Puccini, whose visits to America were not unalloyed pleasure, questioned the costs of embracing the optimistic and ethnocentric dream of improvement, at both a personal and national level.[27] They were questions that would be raised again in the Rodgers and Hammerstein musicals, *South Pacific*, *The King and I* (1951), and *The Flower Drum Song* (1958).

A similar point is made in the next essay, by Carey Wall. Taking seriously the Irving Berlin song made famous by the appropriately stentorian Ethel Merman, "There's No Business Like Show Business," and surveying the musicals which appeared in the years following the success of *Oklahoma!* (1943), Wall looks at the nexus between business and the musical. Focussing closely on Bob Fosse's 1979 film *All That Jazz*, she reveals a problematic relation not unlike that to be found in Puccini's "American" operas. Wall makes use of Geertz's "thick description," and the concept of "communitas," described by his fellow anthropologist Victor Turner. In *Dramas, Fields, and Metaphors*, Turner suggests that communitas "is not shaped by norms" and is not "institutionalized" or "abstract." It consists, rather, in a series of communal relationships which are "spontaneous, immediate, concrete." A modern example cited by Turner is the rescue of Allied troops at Dunkirk in 1940; in doing so he was echoing J. B. Priestley, who in 1941 celebrated Dunkirk as "one of those sudden democratic improvisations."[28] Turner's words suggest that communitas contains elements of the Bakhtinian carnivalesque. As we can see from Wall's analysis, so too do many musicals, creating a genre which mediates the business ethic. They criticise

American culture from an angle of vision not unlike that of the dramas of Arthur Miller. Indeed, some have claimed a more radical status for the musical. The French director Jean-Luc Godard suggested that *The Pajama Game* (directed in 1957 by George Abbott and Stanley Donen), about a strike in a pajama factory, "is the first left-wing operetta." This may be going too far, although, certainly, one of its songs, "This Is My Once A Year Day," presents a Bakhtinian carnival. Furthermore, as Jean-Loup Bourget has pointed out, other musicals contain such elements:

> The musical, like a court jester, is allowed a Saturnalian freedom because it is not a "serious" genre. Its self-eulogy ("Be a Clown" in Minnelli's *The Pirate*, 1948; "Make 'em Laugh" in Donen's and Kelly's *Singin' in the Rain*, 1952; "That's Entertainment" in Minnelli's *The Band Wagon*, 1953) shows its understandable reluctance to part with such a liberty."[29]

The extent to which this liberty is radical is a question for debate. Does the musical attempt to overturn the system, or is it finally reconciliatory?

More direct use of Bakhtin is to be found in Ralph Willett's essay, which is focussed on Hollywood rather than Broadway. In a survey of the forty years from *Gold Diggers of 1933* to *Cabaret* (1972), and looking briefly at the dances of Fred Astaire, Ginger Rogers and Gene Kelly, Willett confirms the point, suggested by Wall's essay, that musicals are not simply "mere escapism"—the phrase normally used to avoid examining them—but rather explorations from within the shifting complexities of a multi-faceted society. He suggests that Busby Berkeley, often regarded as an innovator, was in fact a reactionary figure, his work related to the tightly choreographed production numbers of the impresario Florenz Ziegfeld (1867–1932) and, interestingly, to the production lines of Henry Ford. Willett also confirms the importance of Fosse as a choreographer and director, and his closing comparison of Watergate America with Weimar Germany prompts the thought that Fosse's cultural environment made him the heir of Kurt Weill. Until recently, it has been common to depict Weill's Broadway period as an example of a serious composer selling out. Weill lived in America from 1935 until his death in 1950. The environment of that time resembled neither Weimar nor Watergate. The point is an obvious one, but its implications have yet to be fully explored.[30]

The essays by Mellers, Wall and Willett hint at themes which are worked out in greater detail in the final six essays. That by Anne-Charlotte Hanes Harvey, must through lack of space bear the burden of representing the importance of ethnicity to the musical. Harvey looks at the use of Scandinavian stereotypes in the period from 1900 to 1920, and probes an issue hinted at by Mellers, the cultural friction between the Old World and the New. Most strikingly with the example of "Scandinavian yodelling," Harvey demonstrates that stereotypes, of an Old World which never existed, helped to paper over the fractures created by modernization. Nodding at a famous analysis of the United States in the years immediately prior to American entry into the First World War, Harvey suggests that such stereotypes helped to compensate for the loss of "innocence."[31] By World War II, the threats of modernization had been tamed and innocence had been transformed from a loss into a dream. This would explain why *Oklahoma!*, covering similar ground and revealing once again that nostalgia reconciles the old with the new, nevertheless expresses an ultimately unquestioning vision of modernity. *Oklahoma!* locates the Old World westwards rather than eastwards. One of its stereotypical figures, the cowboy Will Parker, has been east to Kansas City. He has seen the future, and it works. Kansas City, "gas buggies" (as he calls them) and all, remains as a promise that does not threaten the Edenic vision of Oklahoma. This was a view less easily available at the time when the gas buggies were first appearing.

Sue Rickard's essay develops points made by Carey Wall and Ralph Willett. She confirms that the musical is a complex phenomenon which enters into a covert contract with its audience and, concentrating on two Astaire-Rogers dances, "Night and Day" from *The Gay Divorcee* (1934, released in Britain as *The Gay Divorce*), and "Cheek to Cheek" from *Top Hat* (1935), shows that the conditions of censorship of the 1930s allowed Hollywood simultaneously to exploit and deny the erotic potential of dance. Rickard, applying the theories of Bakhtin, suggests that women too can be makers of meaning in a patriarchal society. In doing so she takes a stage further the feminist discussion of the male gaze initiated by Laura Mulvey's well-known essay, "Visual Pleasure and Narrative Cinema."[32] My own essay on *Kiss Me, Kate* covers coarser and clearly misogynistic ground. After surveying critical approaches to Shakespearean film, it attempts to display a dynamic between George Sidney's 1953 film version of Cole Porter's musical and Olivier's 1948 *Hamlet*. It tries also to suggest that Sidney develops the convention of the "backstage musical," discussed briefly by Willett and at length in Jane Feuer's *The Hollywood Musical*, to comment on the cultural conflict between Old and New Worlds, a conflict appropriately resolved by two low-life characters who "brush up their Shakespeare."[33]

The next two essays are examples of the "thicker description" that I mentioned earlier. David Horn shows that two debates which were prompted by George and Ira Gershwin's *Porgy and Bess* (1935)—"the artistic debate" and "the race debate"—could cross forty-four years and the Atlantic to greet the proposal by the Royal Liverpool Philharmonic Society to mount a "community" performance of the text. Horn was present in Liverpool during the debates, and his presence clearly informs his essay. Wilfrid Mellers' second essay has a similar origin, but a different conclusion. As his "Personal Postscript" confirms, Mellers was prompted by a meeting with Leonard Bernstein to reconsider comments about *West Side Story* (1957) that he had made in his groundbreaking 1964 book on American music, *Music in a New Found Land*.[34] In this instance, the passage of time, and the appearance of a new recording conducted by Bernstein himself, had caused him to change his views. This essay therefore forms an important addendum to that book.

The final essay, by Stephen Banfield, looks at the most important current practitioner of the musical and brings us back to the question of aesthetic autonomy. If music operates within a closed aesthetic field then, as Suzanne Langer suggested, the words do not matter. Operating with a relatively new analytical tool, "melopoetics," Banfield explains why lyrics look odd divorced from their proper context, the music, and demonstrates the potency of "Bill," the collaboration of lyricist P. G.

Wodehouse and composer Jerome Kern which finally saw the light of day in *Show Boat*. Stephen Sondheim, of course, is both composer *and* lyricist, and by analyzing songs from *A Funny Thing Happened on the Way to the Forum* (1962), Banfield shows why Sondheim still remains in such high regard, some forty-six years after he first collaborated with Bernstein in *West Side Story*. Although deliberately retaining a close focus, Banfield's discussion hints at contexts other than the immediate one of words. For instance, his reference, in a discussion of the song "Free," to Beethoven's Fifth Symphony, suggests not only the politics which might unite the two composers, but also reminds us of the call-sign used by Allied radio stations during World War II, and of the political capital made during his American career by Arturo Toscanini.[35] His reference to jazz, in a discussion of the dynamic which operates between voice and accompaniments, reminds us that Günther Schuller recently drew attention to the ways that Billie Holiday reshaped—indeed recomposed—popular songs, stamping them indelibly with her voice and changing the course of jazz.[36]

But to develop those contexts would require a much longer book. This one has done enough, I hope, to underline the point recently made by Edward Said:

> ... that the study of music can be more, and not less, interesting if we situate music as taking place, so to speak, in a social and cultural setting. Another way of putting this is to say that the *roles* played by music in Western society are extraordinarily varied... Think of the affiliation between music and social privilege; or between music and the nation; or between music and religious veneration—and the idea will be clear enough...[37]

This book tries to make that idea clearer, and if it persuades the reader of the value of cultural musicological approaches to the American musical, it will have done its job.

NOTES

1 See Richard Kislan, *The Musical: A Look at the American Musical Theater* (Englewood Cliffs, NJ: Prentice-Hall, 1980), pp. 11–7.
2 See Charles Hamm, *Yesterdays: Popular Song in America* (New York: W. W. Norton & Co., 1979), p. 2.

3   See, for instance, Kislan, *The Musical*, pp. 125–7; Cecil Smith and Glenn Litton, *Musical Comedy in America* (2nd ed., New York: Theatre Arts Books, 1981), pp. 157–8; Joseph P. Swain, *The Broadway Musical* (New York: Oxford University Press, 1990), pp. 15–49; and Lawson-Peebles, "Performance Arts," *Modern American Culture: An Introduction*, ed. Mick Gidley (London: Longman, 1993), pp. 279–80.

4   A brief history of the musical is in *The New Grove Dictionary of American Music*, ed. H. Wiley Hitchcock and Stanley Sadie (4 vols., London: Macmillan, 1986), Vol. 3, pp. 289–296.

5   Billie Holiday's "Strange Fruit" (1939), about lynch law in the Southern States, was rejected by major record companies and had to be recorded by a small concern operated by a jazz record store. The remarks in this last and the next paragraph draw on Charles Hamm, *Music in the New World* (New York: W. W. Norton & Co., 1983), pp. 230–42, 340–41, 395–6; David Horn, "Musical America," *Modern American Culture: An Introduction*, ed. Gidley, pp. 239–43; Al Rose, *Eubie Blake* (New York: Schirmer Books, 1979), p. 72; and Robert Kimball and William Balcom, *Reminiscing With Sissle And Blake* (New York: Viking Press, 1973), pp. 9, 133.

6   Hamm, *Yesterdays: Popular Song in America*, pp. 284–6. Isaac Goldberg, *Tin Pan Alley: A Chronicle of American Popular Music* (1930; rpt New York: Frederick Ungar Publishing Co., 1961), p. 33. This point is explored further by David Horn in Chapter 8 below.

7   "Musical comedy," *The New Grove Dictionary of Music and Musicians*, ed. Stanley Sadie (20 vols, London: Macmillan, 1980), Vol. 12, pp. 815–822.

8   Martin Gottfried, *Broadway Musicals* (New York: Harry N. Abrams, Inc., 1979), p. 343.

9   Aristotle, *Poetics*, Ch. 6, "A Description of Tragedy," in *Classical Literary Criticism*, ed. T. S. Dorsch (Harmondsworth, Middlesex.: Penguin, 1965), pp. 38–41.

10 Noel Coward, *Private Lives* (1930; rpt. London: William Heinemann, 1932), p. 30. Glenn Loney, *20th Century Theatre* (2 vols, New York: Facts On File Publications, 1983), I, p. 150.

11 Clement Greenberg, *Art and Culture* (1961; rpt London: Thames and Hudson, 1973), p. 9. Dwight MacDonald, *Against the American Grain: Essays on the Effects of Mass Culture* (1962; rpt New York: Da Capo Press, 1983), pp. 14, 4, 39. For a critique of MacDonald and Greenberg, see Andrew Ross, *No Respect: Intellectuals and Popular Culture* (New York: Routledge, 1989), pp. 42–64.

12 Theodor Adorno and Max Horkheimer, "The Culture Industry: Enlightenment as Mass Deception," *The Cultural Studies Reader*, ed. Simon During (London: Routledge, 1993), pp. 36, 41. Matthew Arnold, *Culture and Anarchy* (1869) and "Civilisation in the United States" (1888), *The Complete Prose Works*, ed. R. H. Super (11 vols, Ann Arbor: University of Michigan Press, 1965, 1977), V, p. 124 and XI, p. 368. As early as 1848, Arnold feared that "American *vulgarity*" would swamp Europe; see *Letters of Matthew Arnold, 1848–1888*, ed. George W. E. Russell (2 vols., London: Macmillan, 1895), I, p. 4. C. E. M. Joad, *The Babbitt Warren* (London: Kegan, French, Trubner, 1926). F. R. Leavis, *Mass Civilisation and Minority Culture* (1930), rpt in *Education and the University: A Sketch for an 'English School'* (London: Chatto & Windus, 1948), pp. 143–71. George Orwell, *Coming Up for Air* (1939; rpt Harmondsworth, Middlesex: Penguin, 1962). Francis Williams, *The American Invasion* (London: Anthony Blond, 1962). A general discussion of European attitudes is given by C. W. E. Bigsby, "Europe, America and the Cultural Debate," *Superculture: American Popular Culture and Europe*, ed. Bigsby (London: Paul Elek, 1975), pp. 1–27.

13 Richard Hoggart, *The Uses of Literacy* (1957; rpt Harmondsworth, Middlesex: Penguin, 1958), pp. 247–50. Production costs of the films mentioned are in Joel W. Finler, *The Hollywood Story* (London: Octopus Books, 1988), pp. 99, 125. Hoggart's complaints are set in context by Dick Hebdige, "Towards a Cartography of Taste 1935–1962," *Block* No 4 (1981), pp. 39–56; Graeme Turner, *British Cultural Studies: An Introduction* (1990; rpt London: Routledge, 1992), pp. 47–51; and Paul Swann, *The Hollywood Feature Film in Postwar Britain* (London: Croom Helm, 1987).

14 Giorgio Vasari, *Lives of the Artists* (1550; trans. and ed. George Bull, Harmondsworth, Middlesex: Penguin, 1965). Walter Pater, *The Renaissance* (1873; rpt ed. Kenneth Clark,

London: Fontana/Collins, 1961), p. 129. Pater's emphasis. Suzanne Langer, *Feeling and Form* (London: Routledge & Kegan Paul, 1953), pp. 152–3.

15 Richard Leppert and Susan McClary, "Introduction," *Music and Society: The Politics of Composition, Performance and Reception*, ed. Leppert and McClary (Cambridge: Cambridge University Press, 1987), p. xii. See also Janet Wolff, "The Ideology of Autonomous Art," *Music and Society*, ed. Leppert and McClary, pp. 1–12.

16 For a brief discussion of the different meanings of "culture," see Raymond Williams, *Keywords: A Vocabulary of Culture and Society* (London: Fontana, 1976), pp. 76–82.

17 Clark Wissler, "Foreword" to Robert S. Lynd and Helen Merrell Lynd, *Middletown: A Study in American Culture* (New York: Harcourt, Brace & Co., 1929), p. vi. Leavis, *Mass Civilisation and Minority Culture* (1930), rpt. in *Education and the University*, pp. 146, 149, 168. On the influence of *Middletown* on the group contributing to the journal *Scrutiny*, see Francis Mulhern, *The Moment of 'Scrutiny'* (London: New Left Books, 1979), pp. 27n, 77, 125, 192 and 192n.

18 Clifford Geertz, "Thick Description: Toward an Interpretive Theory of Culture," in *The Interpretation of Cultures* (New York: Basic Books, 1973), pp. 5, 14. Geertz's critique of Lévi-Strauss see "The Cerebral Savage: On the Work of Claude Lévi-Strauss, *The Interpretation of Cultures*, pp. 345–59.

19 For accounts of the impact of Lévi-Strauss on literary and cultural criticism, see Terence Hawkes, *Structuralism and Semiotics* (London: Methuen, 1977), pp. 32–58; and Ann Jefferson, "Structuralism and Poststructuralism," *Modern Literary Theory: A Comparative Introduction*, ed. Ann Jefferson and David Robey (London: Batsford Academic, 1982), pp. 85–6. For an account of the musicologists' response to Lévi-Strauss and Geertz, see Joseph Kerman, *Contemplating Music: Challenges to Musicology* (Cambridge, MA: Harvard University Press, 1985), pp. 168–81.

20 See, particularly, *Music and the Politics of Culture*, ed. Christopher Norris (London: Lawrence & Wishart, 1989).

21 Theodor Adorno, *Philosophy of Modern Music* (1948), trans. Anne G. Mitchell and Wesley V. Bloomster (London: Sheed & Ward, 1973); *Introduction to the Sociology of Music* (1962), trans. E. B. Ashton (New York: Seabury Press, 1976). Richard Middleton, *Studying Popular Music* (Buckingham: Open University Press, 1990), pp. 34–63. Susan McClary, "The Blasphemy of Talking Politics during Bach Year," *Music and Society*, ed. Leppert and McClary, pp. 13–4. Alastair Williams, "Music as Immanent Critique: Stasis and development in the music of Ligeti," *Music and the Politics of Culture*, ed. Norris, pp. 187–225.

22 Antonio Gramsci, *Selections from the Prison Notebooks*, trans. and ed. Quintin Hoare and Geoffrey Nowell Smith (London: Lawrence & Wishart, 1971). A good introduction to Gramsci's work is James Joll, *Gramsci* (London: Fontana/Collins, 1977). Dick Hebdige, *Subculture: The Meaning of Style* (London: Methuen, 1979), pp. 15–19.

23 Michael Holquist, "Introduction" to M. M. Bakhtin, *The Dialogic Imagination: Four Essays*, trans. Holquist and Caryl Emerson (Austin: University of Texas Press, 1981), p. xxi. Bakhtin's influence is to be found, for instance, in much of *Literary Theory and Poetry: Extending the Canon*, ed. David Murray (London: B. T. Batsford Ltd., 1989); and in Ken Hirschkop, "The Classical and the Popular: Musical Form and Social Context," *Music and the Politics of Culture*, ed. Norris, pp. 283–304.

24 Kerman, *Contemplating Music*, pp. 163–81.

25 The range of Mellers's work is indicated by two titles: *Twilight of the Gods: The Beatles in Retrospect* (London: Faber & Faber, 1973), and "The Heroism of Henry Purcell: Music and politics in Restoration England," *Music and the Politics of Culture*, ed. Norris, pp. 20–40.

26 On immigration and the "melting-pot," see Berndt Ostendorf and Stephan Palmié, "Immigration and Ethnicity," and Lawson-Peebles, "Performance Arts," in *Modern American Culture*, ed. Gidley, pp. 145–50, 262–4.

27 For a brief account of Puccini's relation to the United States, see Benjamin Lawton, "Giuseppe Giacosa and Giacomo Puccini," *Abroad in America: Visitors to the New Nation, 1776–1914*, ed. Marc Pachter and Frances Stevenson Wein (Washington, DC: Smithsonian Institution, 1976), pp. 253–9.

28 Victor Turner, *Dramas, Fields, and Metaphors* (Ithaca, New York: Cornell University Press, 1974), pp. 274, 250–51. J. B. Priestley, *Out of the People* (London: Collins, 1941), p. 8.

29 *Godard on Godard: Critical Writings of Jean-Luc Godard*, ed. Jean Narboni and Tom Milne (London: Secker & Warburg, 1972), p. 86. Jean-Loup Bourget, "Social Implications in the Hollywood Genres," *Film Genre: Theory and Criticism*, ed. Barry K. Grant (Metuchen, NJ: Scarecrow Press, 1977), p. 68.

30 The recent biography by Ronald Taylor, *Kurt Weill: Composer in a Divided World* (1991; rpt London: Simon & Schuster, 1993) has begun the process of setting Weill in his various contexts.

31 Henry F. May, *The End of American Innocence: A Study of the First Years of Our Own Time, 1912–1917* (New York: Knopf, 1969).

32 Laura Mulvey, "Visual Pleasure and Narrative Cinema," *Film Theory and Criticism*, ed. Gerald Mast and Marshal Cohen (3rd ed., New York: Oxford University Press, 1985), pp. 803–16.

33 Jane Feuer, *The Hollywood Musical* (2nd ed., London: Macmillan, 1993).

34 Mellers, *Music in a New Found Land* (London: Barrie and Rockliff, 1964), pp. 428–434.

35 See Joseph Horowitz, *Understanding Toscanini* (1987; rpt Minneapolis: University of Minnesota Press, 1988), particularly pp.117–9, 177–80, 239–40n.

36 Günther Schuller, *The Swing Era: The Development of Jazz 1930–1945* (New York: Oxford University Press, 1989), pp. 527–47.

37 Edward W. Said, *Musical Elaborations* (1991; rpt London: Vintage, 1992), pp. xii, 58.

2

From Butterfly to Saigon: Europe, America, and "Success"

Wilfrid Mellers

When, during the 1990 World Cup, "Nessun Dorma" buzzed in the ears of vast congregations at football stadia throughout Europe, Puccini became Top of the Pops in a sense previously inconceivable. Although his charisma for Italians was indubitable, one would not have anticipated this world-wide dominance. At the start of his career his ambition had been to follow in the footsteps of his hero Verdi, though he lacked Verdi's theatrical ability to create people utterly different from himself. Nor did he possess Wagner's sublime egomania. Less heroically, he knew that to create vital music he had to identify himself with his creatures, and recognized that, since the range of experience that powerfully moved him was limited, he must make do with narrowly stereotyped plots and conventions. He went to considerable pains to persuade his librettists to contrive the kind of situation that interested him; and emerged as a composer who, like Tchaikovsky and Rachmaninov, owes his popular appeal to a psychological, if not overtly pathological, oddness. On reflection this is not surprising, for We the People at once suffer and relish the common maladjustments. Most of us, unable to aspire to Beethovenian or Wagnerian heroism, opt for our petty imperfections.

In the typical Puccini melody, Italian bel canto, shorn of Verdian virility, still soars in stepwise-moving arches but the phrases tend to decline further than they rise. They savor drooping feminine endings, and even split into clauses rounded off by falling fifths. In order to counteract this drooping tendency, Puccini frequently groups his phrases in sequences that *rise*, so that the melodies come out as both limp and hysterically wrought. His more sophisticated harmony, as compared with early and middle period Verdi, emphasizes the subjective emotionalism of his melodies, the more because his partiality for the neutral "Tristan" chords tends to deprive his harmony of momentum. All this, serving to negate the "progressivism" of European music in the eighteenth and nineteenth centuries, suggests that Puccini might be a composer fit for Oswald Spengler's *The Decline of the West* (1926–28)—in which case his preoccupation with non-Western subjects is understandable. One might almost say that he did not evolve these techniques because he chose exotic subjects, but that he dealt with exotic subjects because these were the techniques through which he could say what he had to say.

In his mature work the nervously strained melody, the obsessional, non-directional harmonies and the ostinato rhythm lend themselves readily to the expression of suffering, whether sadistic or masochistic. While such neurotic experience is the genuine element from which Puccini created a language, it may also be the source of a quality inherently synthetic. Having so restricted a range of experience, he is tempted to resort to any expedient to stimulate it; and stimulation may turn into simulation, as his experience becomes self-induced and sentimental because in excess of the subject. This is why Puccini's art, though validly heir to Verdi, also anticipates twentieth-century musical comedy, whether on Broadway or London's The Strand. The element of deceit in his fantasies is one reason for his "fabulous" success.

If *Madama Butterfly* is probably Puccini's finest, as well as his most popular, opera, the reason may be that when it was first produced in 1904 it so potently fused the old type of musical theatre with the new. Its very story is about the clash between an Old World (religious, magical, ancestor-ridden, "pre"-conscious) and a New (forward-looking, scientific, materialistic, militaristic, competitive). Lieutenant Benjamin Franklin

Pinkerton is an American hero who, stationed in distant Japan, thinks he may "for the time being" buy love, as he buys everything else. He is oblivious to the suffering he must cause his Japanese child-bride when, in order to wed a "nice American girl" in his native land, he sunders the marriage-bonds that are, in any case, trivial to him. The failure of Pinkerton (as his blushingly appropriate name may suggest) is perhaps not due to conscious malignity but to lack of imagination, which makes him a very common Tom, Dick or Harry, or you or me. His music is as brashly assertive and as "Western" as the Stars and Stripes anthem that follows him around, and is at the opposite pole to Butterfly's music, which is melodically rooted in non-developing "oriental" pentatonicism and is harmonically root*less* in augmented fifth chords and whole-tone progressions. The collocation of these antithetical musical techniques, as of the two human beings they render audible, can end only in disaster.

Puccini's projection of the social contexts in which his creatures move is as brilliant as his revelation of their identities. The first music we hear is a remorseless fugue in traditionally tragic C major. Its ferocity tells us that we are to witness events that will prove publicly catastrophic, and agonizing in private terms. Yet the music for the first scene, in which Pinkerton interviews the marriage-broker, condescendingly admiring the quaint new buildings and old customs, eschews the overture's grim reality in favor of the anodyne idiom of musical comedy. This makes sense, for the manner of the Market is appropriate to a commodity which, like love, may be bought and sold. Even so, Puccini does not load the dice. It is not a matter of "good" Old Japan against "bad" New America, for although Butterfly is a victim, she is herself vitiated by her impotence, unable to break from her imprisoning world. Suzuki, her companion, represents the positive (religious) aspects of the old tradition; but it appears that Butterfly's father had committed suicide for an unspecified dishonourable act. In the music for the relatives, geisha girls and wedding guests Butterfly-like augmented fifths, swaying irresolutely, sound sinister rather than pathetic. Complementarily, if there is evil in "innocent" Butterfly's world, there is good in "wicked" Pinkerton's, in the person of the kind

21

consul, Sharpless—even though his name may suggest that he does not cut much ice in his society!

Between these two false (because incomplete) worlds is the love-experience of the immature (because stupid) American male and the immature (because childish) Japanese female. *Madama Butterfly* is a great, not merely theatrically effective, opera because its sequence of love scenes grows in depth as the lovers themselves cannot. Butterfly's enthralled first avowal of love is also a capitulation to destiny ("Io segue il mil destino"). In traditionally innocent A major, it significantly precedes the entry of her uncle, the grotesquely furious Bonze, protesting at Butterfly's betrayal of her people. After Pinkerton has brusquely routed the intruders, the A major love song becomes a duet, as the lovers welcome the night ("Viene la sera"). Although Pinkerton here learns to sing butterfly-winged music and they end together on high Cs, the music is no longer in pristine A major, but in F, its flat submediant. The act fades to a dying fall.

The second act opens three years later, with a magical evo-cation of the deserted Butterfly's lonesomeness in her pretty but husbandless home, its coffers empty. Since the pseudo-hero—himself innocent in his obliviousness—is absent, the drama in this act springs from the tension between Suzuki's respect for traditions that are ancestral but moribund, and Butterfly's faithful but bodyless dreams. The big aria in this act is palpable wish-fulfilment ("Un bel di vedremo"), wherein she sees Pinkerton's ship (ironically a grimly grey American warship) bringing him back to her hopeful heart, hearth and home. The key is a very flat and dreamy G flat major, the tune sweetly pen-tatonic, dissolving into rudderless whole-tone haverings. In the "real" world she is wooed by, but rejects, a rich Japanese busi-nessman, who is replaced by, indeed seems to turn into, Sharpless the consul, whose painful duty is to reveal the truth. The stunned silence when Butterfly realizes, but cannot con-sciously accept, this truth is one of the great moments in opera.

It makes possible the genuinely tragic dénouement of the third act, which emerges, by way of the magical "waiting" music, from the amnesiac sleep into which Suzuki, Butterfly and her baby have lapsed in their eternity of non-fulfilment. Pinkerton has returned, in his military machine, bringing his new American wife, intending to claim his and Butterfly's child, to whom he will give a "good American home". It is significant that the third act grows to tragic stature in music from which passively suffering Butterfly is absent. In the magnificent trio ("Io che alle sui penne") Suzuki deplores the enormity of the crimes committed on Butterfly's innocence, Sharpless blunderingly tries to right old wrongs by harping on the child's future, while Pinkerton grows up to the extent of being ravaged by remorse. The remorse is impotent. Butterfly admits that she has no choice but to accept the gods' or God's all too mysterious decree. Her identity seems to collapse in an extraordinary passage of disorientated triads, thinly scored.

But she attains her tragic nemesis when, emulating her father, she kills herself for the dishonor to which she has witlessly been reduced. The opera's final bars are in B minor, traditionally a black key of suffering, as A major was a radiant key of hope. Pinkerton rushes in to fall prostrate over the body of the dying Butterfly who, in the first act, had reminded him that Americans impale butterflies on cards. One cannot know whether Pinkerton's American wife, cozily called Kate, will restore him in his nice American home though, remembering the long sad history of US–Asian relations, one suspects that his rehabilitation must be partial. Puccini's potent music has revealed the burning relevance of this parable in our times, and his opera is far more "modern" than today's musical *Miss Saigon* (1990), which has the same story, more lavish scenic devices, and perhaps an even larger audience, but which has no music that will be alive and kicking ninety years hence.

3

There's No Business Like Show Business: A Speculative Reading of the Broadway Musical

Carey Wall

Cultural analysts like Clifford Geertz, Victor Turner, Mircea Eliade and Erving Goffman show us that no cultural product is merely a commercial transaction; that is, it is more than its sellers bill it. People in the trade know the same thing, but in different terms from those of the cultural analyst. Here is Lehman Engel, long a conductor of Broadway musicals and author of many books aimed at maintaining the vitality of the genre:

> Most of the finest art has been made for a designated space, an occasion, a time, a place, a person, or a purpose. For centuries the best artists learned their livelihoods not by yearning, threatening suicide or feigning epilepsy in an effort to obtain next to impossible materials but by fulfilling precise assignments while utilizing readily available means.[1]

My argument is that the Broadway musical, in its heyday, roughly from *Oklahoma!* (1943) into the early 1960s, mediated America's business ethic and Americans' complex, anxious involvement in that ethic. Business is an *axis mundi* for American culture. On the earthly plane, it keeps American life going, doing everything from getting goods made, shipped and

24

sold, to getting money into people's pockets so they can pay their bills, to making fortunes, small or large. On the heavenly plane, it redistributes money, hence prompting social mobility. On the hellish plane, American business is the local vehicle for human greed, robbery, abuse of others, sharp practice and hidden imperialism of global dimensions. All Americans are involved in multiple ways with business; we participate, reject, acknowledge, give way to, enjoy, hate and jubilate in it. It mediates our relations with other people, for business *is* America. The Broadway musical is the intersection of American arts and American business. The anthem of the Broadway musical— "There's No Business Like Show Business" — tells us that explicitly.

It is worth using Engel's formulation to see the purpose of the Broadway musical. First, the space is those large, central theatres in the largest city of the nation; the theatres to which Americans from the rest of the nation come when they visit the familiar-but-alien power-centre to find their national ethic interpreted. Second, the occasion is that visit to the scene of the nation's power. It is serious, as anything to do with power is; but at the same time it is a vacation to places of entertainment. The entertainments serve, perhaps, in the way the literary device of humour does, screening social verities and so allowing them to be looked at when direct vision is too glaring to be endured. They diffuse and reorient the American's approach to the reality of the place that has been regarded as the heart and pulse of the nation. Third, the time is that of America's international supremacy. Fourth, the place is the whole world, laid open to Americans in the Broadway musical. If it wants the King of Siam, it summons him from the other side of the world. Fifth, the people are all the participants as well as the audiences, all the Americans who know that the business of America is business. Sixth, the purpose is in mediating that cultural anxiety about our relations to others and about ourselves, our humanity, by reason of our choices about doing business.

The Broadway musical I am talking about may be found in histories of the genre but really is timeless, providing Americans with symbols of identity. It is occasionally to be found in revival on Broadway, and Off-Broadway it persists for want of anything better to displace it. The radio no longer broadcasts it, but hundreds of local productions are seasonally entrenched in communities and, at least for middle-aged Americans, for whom the current productions elicit the originals and their times, the Broadway musical play is perpetual in the American scene. It is familiar to large groups of Americans—the songs we know, or recognize, or sing, in whole or in rhythmic snatches, and the names that are radiantly familiar, like Irving Berlin, Rodgers and Hammerstein, Lerner and Loewe, Ethel Merman, Mary Martin, Yul Brynner, Rex Harrison, Agnes De Mille, Jerome Robbins. It is *Oklahoma!*, *South Pacific* (1949), *The King and I* (1951), *Guys and Dolls* (1950), *My Fair Lady* (1956), *The Music Man* (1957), *Carousel* (1945), *Kiss Me, Kate* (1948), *Man of La Mancha* (1965), *West Side Story* (1957), *Fiddler on the Roof* (1964), *Camelot* (1960).

The Connection between Business and the Broadway Musical Play

The connection has many dimensions. There is first the dimension in which show business is itself business. It took big money and significant investment risk to produce the musical, and "hits" were judged only in terms of box-office receipts. It initially served the demands of commerce rather than "art." For the stage-craftsmen and performers, it was unionized work. Like other businesses, show business exploited people in anomalous positions. Agnes De Mille, for instance, writes eloquently in *And Promenade Home* of sharp practices against choreographers.[2] It was early high-tech, uniting several arts and requiring the top specialists in each field. It had the stresses of other high-risk businesses, risking not only money but reputation and predominance. In telling the story of the making of *My Fair Lady*, *Gigi* (1958) and *Camelot*, Alan Jay Lerner reports heart attacks for producer/director Moss Hart and for composer/producer Fritz Loewe; for himself he reports depression and the breakup of several marriages.[3]

Located in business, the musical play interprets business. Sometimes business shows up directly in the plot. Most obviously it appears in *How to Succeed in Business Without Really*

Trying (1961). But it is also to be found in *The Pajama Game* (1954), about a strike in a pajama factory; in *The Music Man*, where conman-salesman "Professor" Harold Hill sells musical instruments by the whole band-load by working the sentiments of small town people; in *Guys and Dolls*, where Nathan Detroit runs a crap-game not for love but for money; in *My Fair Lady*, where Professor Higgins tests his professional reputation; and in *Hello, Dolly* (1964), where Dolly makes marriages, including her own, for financial security.

Furthermore, business and the musical play of this period share a number of common characteristics. Business is full of risks and, sometimes, rewards. In the musical, the plots frequently show people taking risks, in the form of leaps into the unknown. In *South Pacific* (1949), Lieutenant Cable takes a Malaysian girl as his sweetheart and Nellie Forbush finds that the perfect man of her enchanted evening has Eurasian children. In *My Fair Lady* Eliza Doolittle has to leap from the culture of low-expectations her surname indicates into the demanding, manipulative culture of sophistication. In *Oklahoma!* (1943) Laurie's leap from autonomous girl into no-longer-autonomous wife parallels and interprets her community's leap into the society-making of a "brand new state." Sometimes it is simply the leap of a small-town girl coming to the big city (*Wonderful Town*, 1953); sometimes it is the leap across racial barriers in defiance of death (*West Side Story, 1957*). Of course, such leaps are the stuff of plots; but they are plots capable of many shifting nuances, worked to respond to the needs of the particular culture, and the nuances give us what Clifford Geertz calls "thick description."[4] The Broadway musical shades and shapes its characters' story-generic leaps, I believe, to make them parallel the leaps Americans must perform in doing business.

The chief reward of show business is success, and the reward is not precisely calculable. It is a quality, something with an aura. It is stardom. Success—success in love, success in achieving stardom, the two conjoined and the conjunction giving the aura to success—is the result of the musical play's plot. Just as business is imperialistic, so the Broadway musical play is imperialistic, knowing no geographical boundaries to the stories it can use to turn into dollars. The King of Siam (in *The King and I*) is joined by the English language professor and the Cockney layabout scoundrel and his daughter (*My Fair Lady*), and European Jews at the moment of their emigration (*Fiddler on the Roof*). While much of its material is wholly American, it is characteristic of the genre to reach for non-American material that can be treated in the same terms. There is success in turning the unfamiliar into the familiar, the known, part of the American musical.

I will return to some of these points. Here, my argument about the connection between business as an anxiety node in American culture and the Broadway musical play lies in a relationship between the stuff of private lives (mostly what the musicals present us with) and business as the public dimension of American personality. Musicals usually begin with a "Beautiful Mornin'" and end with what Victor Turner, in *Dramas, Fields, and Metaphors*, called "communitas." The triumph of good feelings is what the musicals give us, what they make us happy about. In contrast, our commitment to business makes us anxious about our ability to achieve communitas, for business is well-known for demoting human bonds to a lower priority. Business works, in large part, by alienating the connections between people that might get in the way of the profit motive. There are, of course, familial and other circles within which business is distributed and into which outsiders cannot break. But these are "hidden" operations. The "avowed" is that personal relations may not upset business because business is too important; hence our anxiety. If business is assigned the public-self function, then everything about personal relationships is left for the private-self function, and the two are inalienably connected.

The keynote of the Broadway musical is energy. It varies from other musical modes in America chiefly by virtue of that specially nuanced energy, associated, among other things, with the identifiable sound of the pit-band. Business, too, is American energy, welling up endlessly from our belief in our newness in world history, and organizing our lives both inside our borders and with the world at large. Lehman Engel notes that most Broadway hits have books that are not original but adaptations of extant fiction, drama or movies;[5] in other words, the Broadway musical offers and tests a treatment of material. So too does business; it offers a treatment of the relationship between people and the goods and services that support life.

Greater Depth: The Avowed and the Hidden

I have already borrowed the terms "avowed" and "hidden" from Richard Sykes, who points out that in analyzing culture we must expect the hidden as well as the avowed:

> An *avowed pattern* is one which is publicly practiced and expressly recognized by those who practice it. It is usually legal and openly approved.... A *masked pattern* has at least some of the following characteristics: It is seldom openly discussed or publicly sanctioned, though it may be admitted in intimate groups. In some cases it is masked because the members of a culture do not realize that it is a generally shared pattern. In some cases virtually all members of a culture may be unaware that any pattern exists, not because it is consciously hidden, but because it ... is too habitual to be noticed. In some cases a pattern may be masked because it is repressed. Members of a culture may feel anxious about a particular danger or threat, but fear to admit their anxiety. Members of a culture may feel a kind of unmet need, but be unable to verbalize it. Often a masked culture pattern exists because it contradicts an already avowed pattern. Masked patterns must often be isolated by undirect means.[6]

The avowed/hidden duality is the cultural arrangement by which we privilege some of our knowledge and allow expression of knowledge we have forbidden ourselves. We need expression of forbidden knowledge to keep in touch with it, so that we do not deceive ourselves about the nature of reality, for in that deception we would lose control. Knowing what we agree we do not know, we remain in the position of choice, choosing, for instance, to do business even though we know it has hellish dimensions. Cultural artifacts reveal implications and facets, allow us to see our choices and to choose to reaffirm them or make changes. In short, they serve what Victor Turner calls liminal purposes, putting axioms to the test so that we can see whether they still hold good.[7] The Broadway musical play shows us the dimensions of American business, and gives us the satisfaction of examining its depth. Not that we are aware of all this; consciousness, in fact, breaks some of the effectiveness. The popular arts work the unconscious more than the conscious and; their form is one that stylizes, conventionalizes, so that what is hot in its materials can be taken coolly.

It is important to recognize that the hidden is not off-stage, invisible. Hidden does not mean out of sight; it means, exactly, not seen when in full view, not acknowledged though present. The way to see the hidden is to shift one's perspective, to look obliquely rather than directly. When one looks at the Broadway musical in this fashion, every element contributes to duality. Avowed optimism, hidden anxiety. Avowed, the capacity for universal love, the ability to cross boundaries and embrace all people; hidden, universality as a screen for refusal to recognize genuine cultural differences and preferences.

The Avowed/The Full Self

The popular arts are of course active in the realm of cultural mythology, and the myth of the businessman is the one that needs to be retrieved here. Business characteristically precludes and demotes the values of family, friendship, sharing, except insofar as teamwork makes them valuable to the company and its profits. In business, it is every man for himself. That is the smart way, the successful way, the way that produces the profits which are the goal of business. In crises the businessman is expected to (and perhaps does) choose business necessity over minor family crisis. When competition and friendship conflict, competition for profit is supposed to demand the businessman's adherence to the faith. Just as Mark Twain's *Adventures of Huckleberry Finn* demonstrates that educated, cultivated, free Americans living under an avowed doctrine of equality cannot make Black people slaves without having to suppress their guilt,[8] so the Broadway musical demonstrates American anxiety about the truncated self. If the self is truncated, then Americans are guilty of refusing help to people who have helped them (self-help being a myth rather than fact) and, as well, of abusing the full life that America

30

was "invented" to develop. The Broadway musical allays that anxiety by recovering the full self.

Critics of the Broadway musical distinguish the musical play from the musical comedy; the musical play involves serious drama, leaving frivolities behind.[9] However, the distinction is a superficial one, for comedy is essentially an action of renewal, and may or may not be associated with frivolity. The musical play is perhaps richer, but remains comic in its action of renewal, which is first announced by its energy. No energy, of whatever style, no hit. Energy implies health, and the wholeness that emerges in health. Singing in the musical play has its required sweet, lyrical moments, but the range has a special place for Ethel Merman and the raucous way she belts out the words.

Performing gets rid, to a notable extent, of the gendered division of energies, regarded as normal in daily (and business) life. In musicals masculinity and femininity are removed to roles while the performers extend themselves, the men costuming themselves (which, in a business culture, only women could do) and the women developing a muscularity necessary for dancing and for compelling movement on the large stage. Certainly, performers are cast for their gender-specific bodily appearance, but once on stage they are all, in unisex style, working. In presenting song and dance, the musical play recovers functions and expression precluded in business precincts. No one wins a contract for his company by singing an aria. Song and dance are quite different from the speaking, walking, sitting and posturing to which business people are confined. Business is in the grip of history, to the individual difference of each deal, each sales season. Song and dance represent freedom, are repositories of conventions that record yet extend our lyricism, and deny the limitation of the body to daily routine motions.[10] Song and dance recover a very great deal with the greatest economy of means.

The plots make individual characters triumph. The star-system makes us aware of the star as much as of the character; and in that stardom which brings applause at the first entrance on the stage we see the self approved, magnified, validated. For the shows are vehicles for stars already made or in the making. The plots exaggerate the presence that stardom establishes.

They present the individual self against great forces, the self now large enough to stand up in opposition to those forces. In this fashion the musical overlaps culturally with the Western, which has been seen to retrieve the self from the anonymity into which business conditions plunge it.[11] More importantly, self and success are reunited. Unlike business, which is divisive, setting the businessman against his competitors and anyone else who can be hurt in sharp dealing, the musical play, dealing with the otherworld of human relationships, finds the star-self a place to shine, to enjoy, and not to hurt others.

In fact, the structural conventions of the musical mine the traditions and implications of comedy to carry the self over into communitas. The plot ends with the conventional comic reintegration of society, uniting all, and the Broadway stage fills to fullness, with song, with soaring dance, with casts that crowd the stage, its final moment reminding us of everything that has happened since the curtain went up. Stars and supporting cast link arms and raise their voices together; communitas defeats hierarchy among the performers. Song and dance, augmented from their beginnings in the opening scenes, have developed sufficiently to suggest further development, if not within the boundaries of the material of that particular plot, then in future musicals. For the musical is something to which fans go as "a musical" as much as to see the latest incarnation with the latest stars. In contrast to the genres where difference matters tremendously, each hit musical evokes all the others we know, augmenting rather than diminishing audience experience. One musical evokes others to our satisfaction more, I think, than any novel does by evoking other novels.

It is all of this, I think, to which commentators on the musical allude. Critic Richard Kislan (who is also widely experienced as a practitioner in the field) argues:

> Musical theater is romantic popular theater, a theater of all the people. Where reason eludes the mob, strong emotion does not.... the majority of smash-hit musicals in the classic musical theater repertory feature the wisely crafted, romantic-sentimental book that gives the audience an opportunity to share universal feeling, to laugh and sigh and cry together. They scramble the shared emotions of the

audience, then resettle them. If the audience smiles deeply as it leaves the theater, it smiles less out of relief than out of recognition of a shared humanity experienced in a collective act of involuntary emotional response. The romantic-sentimental book tells the audience: you *feel*, therefore you *are*— and it is good.[12]

That is what I mean in speaking of the recovery of the self.

If the audience gets communitas out of a wonderful performance of an American musical play, so, Leonard Bernstein testifies, can its makers. Here he speaks of the opening of *West Side Story*, repeating the point made by Lehman Engel at the beginning of this essay, but going beyond it:

> The opening last night was just as we dreamed it. All the agony and postponements and re-re-rewriting turn out to have been worth it. There's a work there; and whether it finally succeeds or not in Broadway terms, I am now convinced that what we dreamed all these years *is* possible; because there stands that tragic story, with a theme as profound as love versus hate, with all the theatrical risks of death and racial issues and young performers and "serious" music and complicated balletics— and it all added up for audience and critics. I laughed and cried as though I'd never seen or heard it before. And I guess that what made it come out right is that we really all *collaborated*; we were all writing the *same* show. Even the producers were after the same goals we had in mind. Not even a whisper about a happy ending was heard. A rare thing on Broadway. I am proud and honored to be part of it.[13]

The Hidden

In quoting this passage from Bernstein, I have already begun my section on the hidden, for Bernstein is moved both by the experience of collaboration (the italics are his) and by the audience's and critics' acceptance of tragedy within the form of the musical play. Tragedy is that dark side of life that "entertainment" (often bracketed with "light" as "light entertainment") seeks to exclude as a trespasser with no rights. But life is shallow without recognition of tragedy. Tragedy gives life high value, and Bernstein, bringing his music to the point where it intersects with the dominant business ethic, is tremendously satisfied that he can achieve a conjunction of the upbeat and the sensitive dimensions of life.

Writer and director Moss Hart, speaks in similar terms:

> I suspect that today's bland dismissal of the intellectual and the overwhelming emphasis placed on the necessity of competing and of success are due in part to the strange taboo we have set against that softness in ourselves which brings men closest to the angels. A nation of poets would be no more desirable than a nation of athletes, but I wonder if that toughness and competitiveness, which have become an ingrained part of our character as a people and a symbol of our way of life as a nation, are not a sign of weakness as well as of strength. Is our cultural life not robbed of a necessary dimension and our emotional life of an element of grace? And I wonder if the fear of a lack of toughness in our children does not sometimes rob them of an awakening awareness and sensitivity in the realm of the spirit that are each child's birthright and his weapon of rebellion against the accepted norm of his time. This lack of toughness and the inability to compete were a constant agony of my own childhood, and I lived it through as best I could.[14]

The shape of Hart's statement emphasizes the musical's recovery function and suggests how to deal with anxieties. The musical avows optimism; it shouts "we can do it." At the centre of all its affirmations is the one Ethel Merman sings about in "There's No Business like Show Business:"

> Yesterday they told you you would not go far
> That night you open and there you are
> Next day on your dressing room they've hung a star
> Let's go on with the show.

"You" here are character/actor/audience/America; in the musical you are transformed overnight in this American version of "Once upon a time" from any-ordinary-body into the star.

> Ev'rything about it is appealing
> Ev'rything the traffic will allow
> No-where can you get that happy feeling,
> When you are stealing that extra bow.[15]

It is a terrific high that Merman sings about. I say Merman because although Irving Berlin wrote it she is thoroughly identified with the song. When anyone else sings it, Merman is evoked singing behind the performer. The power of this affirmation makes possible disclosure of the anxieties that in everyday business we hide.

The avowal is potent because the techniques of the musical are brought to feed on something like "human truth" or "true feeling" in the source texts which they adapt. Moss Hart says that the audience can distinguish the false from the true;[16] the "fit" between the musical treatment and the original material is probably what the audience is finding false or true. The audience does not have to know the original text in order to perform this act of judgment. The character types, each with an attached network of values and shades of feeling, that are to be found in Thornton Wilder's *The Matchmaker* (source material for *Hello, Dolly*) or Ferenc Molnar's *Liliom* (source material for *Carousel*) or George Bernard Shaw's *Pygmalion* (source material for *My Fair Lady*) or any of the other sources are also to be found elsewhere in the culture. The sources and their derivatives tap into a cultural continuum of character roles which the audience will have learned. Wherever the musical's treatments *extend* the originals without violating them, all the human truth contained in the original bursts out onto the musical stage. As Alan Jay Lerner said of *My Fair Lady*, "we finally arrived at those moments where music and lyrics could reveal what was implied and not repeat what was already in the text, and could catch the drama at the hill-tops where it could ascend no farther without the wings of music and lyrics."[17]

The avowal gets so much strength in this manner that it can sustain optimism while demons come forth to be exorcized, or merely to be acknowledged by the audience before they slip out of sight—until the next musical. All the demons spring from a single sire: the need to succeed. Of course, American culture is not monolithic. Victor Turner paraphrases the art critic Harold Rosenberg, arguing that "the culture of any society at any moment is more like the debris, or 'fall-out,' of past ideological systems, than it is itself a system, a coherent whole."[18]

Nevertheless, the business ethic has roots in enough past systems to prevail upon anyone susceptible to internalizing the message: "Don't be a fool. Do business. Make something of yourself. Succeed." One of the demons is frantic movement: singing and dancing almost non-stop, singing and dancing even when one knows the voice is off-key and the body is too untrained or too tired to hold the controlled form that is dance. Agnes De Mille's autobiography, *Dance to the Piper*, is one account of just such frenzy.[19] The musical regulates this movement, transforming it into the formed, the ordered, the meaningful, the successful.

Lack of success makes Americans empty, invisible. If race does this to Black Americans (as Ralph Ellison suggests in his 1952 novel *Invisible Man*), then they get doubly what white Americans get in their own fashion when they internalize the business ethic, for business tends to blossom nightmarishly, becoming everything. When there is no success, there are no alternative satisfactions. There is simply nothing. The Broadway musical play lies at many leagues' distance from *Moby Dick*, but the demon of failure is as potent a threat in the musical as it is to Captain Ahab. The musical fills the stage, creating the full moment that is, for the time being, enough to exorcize the demon of emptiness and return Americans to the fullness in which the self can breathe again.

Doing business makes Americans vultures, or makes us fear that we may be vultures. Here, the musical makes use of comedy's acknowledgement of death to kill the vulture. It kills the vulture in two ways. The communitas it invokes reveals our humanity. It also places communitas at a distance by revealing its limits. *Camelot* is the highest expression of this distancing, but other examples are to be found in *Brigadoon*, *Man of La Mancha* and *Paint Your Wagon*, or wherever nostalgia and other yearning after what is lost occurs. Musicals affirm what ought to have been; they give high importance to those values to which we aspire.

Perhaps there are further revelations in the musical. Perhaps some part of the audience recognizes that the apparent universality by which we bring characters from other parts of the world into our American communitas is a spatial rather than a cultural movement. There is little acknowledgement of genuine cultural differences and the compromises they necessitate. Instead, universality is a kind of conservatism, a mask for the procedure of converting everything to American terms. Jerome Robbins universalized Siam in *The King and I* by his parallel between Harriet Beecher Stowe's *Uncle Tom's Cabin* and "The Small House of Uncle Thomas." Ethnocentricity is in no way exorcized; for those who can see it, it merely pokes out a pale face from behind the stars serenading their roots. The wish-fulfillment, in this instance, is that a certain coarseness be acceptable, the coarseness captured by Ethel Merman's voice when she belts out a song in the Broadway idiom, as Leonard Bernstein points out, "so full of jazz."[20] Ethnocentricity is just part of that gravel, that urban hardness. It looms small and we forgive it, if we see it, in the magnitude of the musical's liberated joy. It is left to other arts to mediate more powerfully our ethnocentricity. It is enough for the Broadway musical to return us to our feeling.

Choosing the Musical: Bob Fosse and All That Jazz

In *America Dances*, Agnes De Mille calls Bob Fosse's 1979 film *All That Jazz* "a most extraordinary treatment in parable and metaphor of the current dilemma of the successful stage personality."[21] I will argue that the "successful stage personality" belongs to the makers of the musical, to America, and to the audience as well as to stars like the film's Joe Gideon.

Choreographer/director Bob Fosse had more credits on Broadway than in Hollywood, although he made the film versions of several of his Broadway successes, *The Pajama Game* (1954), *Damn Yankees* (1958), *Sweet Charity* (1969), and *Cabaret* (1972). He also choreographed on Broadway *Bells Are Ringing* (1956), *New Girl in Town* (1957) (based on Eugene O'Neill's *Anna Christie*; another example of serious material brought to Broadway), *Redhead* (1959), *How to Succeed in Business Without Really Trying* (1961), *Little Me* (1962), *Pippin* (1972), *Chicago* (1975), and *Dancin'* (1978). He directed nearly half of these shows as well. When he came to his heart attack and to *All That Jazz*, then, he created an autobiography as well

37

as an interpretation of the Broadway musical. Fosse began his involvement in Broadway in the period which I have been discussing, but he was of a younger generation than the creators of *Oklahoma!* (1943), and the list of his credits announces, along with his career, the move into different times. There was clear continuity in Fosse's work from the charming "Steam Heat" and "Hernando's Hideaway" of *The Pajama Game* to "Air-Rotica" of *All That Jazz*, and this continuity contributes to my argument about "the hidden" in the musical in its prime. The shift to more recent times, as indicated in Fosse's works, is from the bright toward the dark. There is greater recognition of the rough, the coarse, the cannibalistic.

This shift derives less from any natural maturation of the form, I should think, than from the shift in America's position in the world in the last two decades. Americans can no longer ascribe to a mythology of a nation happily supreme in world markets and cultural virtue as they apparently did in the days of *Oklahoma!* (1943) and *West Side Story* (1957). As America's image becomes tarnished in its citizens' eyes, the musical—supremely in *All That Jazz*—takes full measure of the damage done by show business. Nevertheless, its charm holds, or proves unsurrenderable. Joe Gideon has to make a choice in the musical and, rather than choosing discretion and longer life on lesser and simpler terms, he goes "on with the show."

The name Gideon brings to mind the Bible, and indeed show business is the Bible to this man. In making shows he preaches show business's gospel to others. It is, by 1979, a shaky gospel, a gospel of joy on the edge where joy is suddenly convertible to self-destruction. At the top of the show biz field, Gideon is trying to do too much. The gospel of the musical is what he has internalized. Believing in that larger, unconquerable self the musical created, he tries to make his more limited real person do all the exalted self can do. This crossover is impossible. As the film opens Gideon is keeping himself going on showers, eye drops, amphetamines, booze, cigarettes, alka seltzer, sex, competitiveness, and the phrase, "It's show time, folks." His genuine artistry can sustain this abuse, but his private self cannot. The women who love him despite his errant ways (his ex-wife Audrey, his daughter Michelle, and his girlfriend Katy) belong to the tradition of the musical in its confident prime; but he cannot come together or stay with any of them. He has internalized the frenzied movement that the musical used to be able to contain. Show biz folk, according to the hyperbolical conventions of the media, are entertainers, humanitarians, and friends. But when, towards the end, O'Connor Flood, the mordant Black comedian played by Ben Vereen, introduces Gideon for his last performance on the stage of life, he varies the formula, voicing Gideon's discouragement, calling him "a so-so entertainer, not much of a humanitarian, and nobody's friend." Gideon is discouraged because, in his own words, he can't tell where "reality leaves off and the bullshit begins." He doesn't know if he loves anyone; instead, he knows he believes in saying, "I love you." It does the business, gets him the sex with women he wants.

Gideon is not cut off from all feeling or perspective. Sequences about the character Vicki, a show-biz-struck girl who wants to be a star and has the looks but does not dance very well, reveal something of Gideon's humanity. In one, he tells her, gently as well as brutally, that he does not think she will become a star. In another, Gideon makes the girl face her limitations as a dancer and then takes time out to encourage her not to quit, but rather to work to get better, promising her that while he cannot make her a fine dancer, he can make her a better one. Here is a 1979 variation of the older musical's breakthrough into goodness and communitas, diminished in proportion within the whole network of realities that are show biz.

Looming much larger in *All that Jazz* are the importance of money, and the inexorable, impossible pace, the competition, and the limits of the living self, vulnerable as well to the reviews which are the vehicle for that passion to destroy the successful that comes from the public rather than immediate competitors. Gideon dies in *All That Jazz*. Fosse himself survived that particular heart attack, but carried the logic of his material to its inevitable conclusion. The foe of show business is mortality; not hate, not prejudice, not novelty that can disorient or overwhelm, not the inability of human beings to sustain their ideals, but simply mortality. In the scenes featuring Ben Vereen, Fosse effectively displays the five stages in approaching death, outlined in 1969 by Elisabeth Kübler-Ross following work in Chicago: denial, anger, bargaining, depression, acceptance.[22] Once again the musical/business/America nexus allows the musical to interpret America's position and the faith of its citizens.

Both Gideon and Flood can find no credible correspondence between the self and the reality of human mortality. In the end, although he accepts death, Gideon's faith remains with the show business ethic of transcendence. Despite harsh words from his doctor and pleas from Audrey, Katy and Michelle, he mixes up death, somewhat deliberately, somewhat confusedly, with another encounter with a beautiful woman. She appears to him periodically throughout the film, a woman in white. Fosse here gives signs of knowing American literary history. His use of whiteness in *All that Jazz* renews and extends that literary symbol, whose centrepiece is "The Whiteness of the Whale" in *Moby Dick*. Gideon, dying, moves towards the looming figure the woman in white has now become, reminding us of the closing entries in Edgar Allan Poe's *The Narrative of Arthur Gordon Pym*, where the boat is driven inexorably towards the "shrouded human figure" whose skin "was of the perfect whiteness of the snow." This moment in the film also recalls Emily Dickinson's "Because I could not stop for Death—/He kindly stopped for me."[23] The woman in white is there for the purpose of leading Gideon across the boundaries between two worlds. She symbolizes the transformative power that, unexhausted, converts Gideon's death from further heart attacks into a last performance on the stage of life that lies in the redemptive, communitas plane of earlier musicals. Here, everyone Gideon knows is assembled in the audience, while Gideon (with Flood playing Jim to Gideon's Huckleberry Finn) makes his farewells, making peace with everyone, defining himself in this last appearance as the flawed but joy-giving man who spent his life's energy in making musicals.

Fosse shows us Gideon's corpse zipped into the body-bag. The reality of Gideon's time in the hospital (including shots of open-heart surgery), however, is thoroughly worked into the musical matrix. Gideon and an orderly do a little, repeated rendition of "Pack Up Your Troubles in Your Old Kit Bag and Smile, Smile, Smile." What *is* the use of worrying? Busby Berkeley and the whole tradition of the Hollywood musical (of which *All that Jazz* is one of the greatest exemplars) are evoked in the production number of "After You've Gone." Such numbers give rich range and shading to the charm of the musical's transformative force as it overwhelms, not mortality, of course, but the importance and credibility of mortality. *All That Jazz* registers all the difference in the America of 1979, but it also registers America's adherence to its faith. There is more affirmation than irony when, as we see the dead body zipped into the bag, and the closing credits appear in white, we hear Merman sing "There's No Business Like Show Business."

Conclusion

When Clifford Geertz puts together his persuasive and evocative explication of the cockfight and its role in Balinese culture, he deals with adjacent, concurrent and abutting vortices of action that are part of the whole phenomenon, the web of relationships, that goes by the simple name, "the cockfight."[24] The Broadway musical obviously has its own entanglements of contributory phenomena invisible in this sketchy discussion. They must include such things as the American perspective of New York as a world centre during the period of the musical in its prime; the demographically disproportionate participation of Jewish people in the creation of the musical, using the genre to transform themselves from outsiders to insiders, intimates at the very centre; and the export of New York to the American provinces via road shows and local productions of this Broadway form. Even without present discussion of these and many other attendant parts of the Broadway musical's cultural action, I think it is possible to leap to the provisional conclusion that in the Broadway musical we have a cultural product quite deliberately (if hiddenly) manipulated to replicate the laws of the mythology of American business. Broadway productions do not have to be hits or flops with no middle ground between, though those who spend their lives in the business clearly believe that this phenomenon is God-sent rather than man-made. Business does not have to be run in a fashion that either obtains its participants' top priority or charges them with apostacy. It is not money but rather cultural allegiances that create this demand, which is passed from generation to generation as powerfully as are sex roles. Such statistical measurements as Gross National Product, balance of trade figures, megatrends, and so on, prove that Americans commit and recommit themselves to business. The Broadway musical approaches the commitment from a specific angle of vision, and, like the role of the cockfight in Balinese culture, provides us with an encounter with that commitment, and the anxieties and faith on which it rests.

NOTES

1 Lehman Engel, *Words with Music* (New York: Macmillan, 1972), p. 3.

2 Agnes De Mille, *And Promenade Home* (Boston: Little, Brown, 1958), pp. 250–60.

3 Alan Jay Lerner, *The Street Where I Live: The Story of My Fair Lady, Gigi and Camelot*, pp. 112–3, 183–6, 194–6.

4 Clifford Geertz, *The Interpretation of Cultures* (New York: Basic Books, 1973), pp. 3–30.

5 Engel, *Words with Music*, p. 6.

6 Richard Sykes, "American Studies and the Concept of Culture: A Theory and Method," *American Studies: Essays on Theory and Method*, ed. Robert Merideth (Columbus, Ohio: Merrill, 1968), pp. 78–79.

7 Victor Turner, *Dramas, Fields, and Metaphors* (Ithaca, New York: Cornell University Press, 1974), p. 255.

8 See Carey Wall, "The Boomerang of Slavery: The Child, the Aristocrat, and Hidden White Identity in *Huckleberry Finn*," *Southern Studies* 21 (Summer 1982), pp. 208–21.

9 See, for instance, Martin Gottfried, *Broadway Musicals* (New York: Harry N. Abrams, Inc., 1979); and Richard Kislan, *The Musical: A Look at the American Musical Theater* (Englewood Cliffs, NJ: Prentice-Hall, 1980).

10 This modality is taken from Mircea Eliade, "Freedom and History," *The Myth of the Eternal Return*, trans. Willard R. Trask (London: Routledge & Kegan Paul, 1955), pp. 154–9.

11 See Will Wright, *Sixguns and Society: A Structural Study of the Western* (Berkeley: University of California Press, 1975), particularly pp.173–84.

12 Richard Kislan, *The Musical: A Look at the American Musical Theater* (Englewood Cliffs, NJ: Prentice-Hall, 1980), pp. 173–4.

13 Leonard Bernstein, "Excerpts from a West Side Story Log," *Findings* (New York: Simon and Schuster, 1982), pp. 146–7. In this passage he may be speaking of the new American music he expected to emerge from the musical play; see Bernstein, "American Musical Comedy," *The Joy of Music* (New York: Simon and Schuster, 1959), pp. 152–79.

14 Moss Hart, *Act One: An Autobiography* (New York: Random House, 1959), p. 30.

15 Irving Berlin, "There's No Business Like Show Business," *The Golden Years of Irving Berlin* (London: Chappell, n.d.), pp. 82–7.

16 Hart, *Act One*, p. 74.

17 Lerner, *On the Street Where I Live*, p.45.

18 Turner, *Dramas, Fields, and Metaphors*, p. 14.

19 Agnes De Mille, *Dance to the Piper* (Boston: Little, Brown, 1952).

20 Bernstein, *The Joy of Music*, p. 172.

21 Agnes De Mille, *America Dances* (New York: Macmillan, 1980), p. 200.

22 Elisabeth Kübler-Ross, *On Death and Dying* (1969; rpt. London: Routledge, 1989), pp. 34–121.
23 Edgar Allan Poe, *The Narrative of Arthur Gordon Pym* (Harmondsworth, Middlesex: Penguin, 1975), p. 239. Emily Dickinson, *The Complete Poems*, ed. Thomas H. Johnson (London: Faber & Faber, 1970), No. 712, p. 350.
24 Clifford Geertz, "Deep Play: Notes on the Balinese Cockfight," *The Interpretation of Cultures*, pp. 412–53.

4

From Gold Diggers to Bar Girls: A Selective History of the American Movie Musical

Ralph Willett

The musical film is the most representative Hollywood product, both celebrating myths central to the industry and re-affirming the position of entertainment in the imaginative life of its audience. While embedded in the tradition of show business song and dance, it is also about entertainment in a self-justificatory way. In the words of Jane Feuer, "all Hollywood films sought to be entertaining, but the musical could incorporate a myth of entertainment into its aesthetic discourse."[1] The product consequently contains a binary message. On the one hand, the musical uses show business as a utopian metaphor of society. Life should, it suggests, aspire to the conditions of theatrical performance, and it makes such possibilities plausible by presenting images of naturalness, ease, and pleasure. On the other hand, the musical's awareness of the restrictions and burdens of social reality demands the creation of alternatives, of ways of escaping the contemporary. Busby Berkeley's film productions provide good examples of the movie musical's ambivalent nature. In *42nd Street*, for instance, a series of opulent, fantastic dances at the film's climax represents an expressionistic release from the Depression-ravaged USA of 1933, the year of the movie's distribution. However, the final image presents the figure of the lonely, ageing show director, Julian Marsh, slumped on the steps in the theatre's alley outside; a downbeat, sombre ending at odds with the preceding sequences.

42nd Street, like Berkeley's other films from this period, *Gold Diggers of 1933* and *Footlight Parade* (1933), is a backstage musical. Over half the musicals ever made, including such recent examples as *Cabaret* (1972) and *Fame* (1980), fall into this category, which combines at least three interrelated forms and devices. First, putting on a show enables the theatrical community to renew itself through the ultimate success of performance, triumphing over such human vices as greed and egotism. Typically, backstage musicals have a temperamental star who must learn to think of others. Sometimes, musicals address wider social problems. In the case of *Gold Diggers of 1933*, it is the Great Depression which is vanquished by a backstage team which, pulling together, acts as a model for the attempts of the wider community to turn America around economically. Second, the backstage musical merged the communal ethic with individualism and with the romantic story of young love. A frequent plot device, as in both *Broadway Melody of 1936* and *Broadway Melody of 1938*, presents a small-town girl who hopes to break into show business on Broadway. Sexual and artistic energy provide the dynamics of form; they run parallel but converge in the final performance, the success of the artists on stage sealing their romance, guaranteeing their happiness as lovers. In this instance, however, *Gold Diggers of 1933* does not run true to type. The couple, played by Dick Powell and Ruby Keeler, does not perform in the finale, "My Forgotten Man." The original intention was to have the film end with them together in "Shadow Waltz," Powell also appearing with Joan Blondell in "We're in the Money." The final version perhaps represents a conscious decision to emphasize communality and the grim details of the Depression. Third, singing and dancing are presented as professional activity. In the two *Broadway Melodies* Eleanor Powell (no relation to Dick) succeeds because she is the most dedicated to her art. In Busby Berkeley's films, however, this "realism" is subverted by the inventiveness and mobility of his camerawork which transparently goes beyond standard theatrical limits.

Pre-Berkeley musicals were often filmed versions of Broadway shows. Berkeley's spectacular numbers, too, derive from the richly extravagant revues and stage presentations such as the *Ziegfeld Follies* (1944). As Babington and Evans phrase it, "the rarified girlie show" of the earlier revues was transformed by Berkeley into "a carnivalesque riot of unfettered images."[2] In using the term "carnivalesque," Babington and Evans indicated that they were drawing on the insights of the Soviet critic Mikhail Bakhtin, who suggested that the function of laughter was parodic, a life-enhancing debunking of the solemnity of official culture.[3] Berkeley, though, was no revolutionary spirit despite the apparent homage to surrealism in his ensembles. It could be argued that the modernist elements in his musicals are cancelled out, as entertainment is celebrated through the unifying set-piece which concludes each show (and movie). Berkeley's choreographed routines, so far from suggesting liberation, as many later musicals do, display the characteristics of mass production and standardized behavior found typically in the industrial systems of Henry Ford. As Bruce Norman has shown, there is a striking similarity between a production line and, for instance, the massed pianos (with their lookalike players) in *Gold Diggers of 1935*.[4] Indeed, the pedigree of the large-scale, voyeuristic tableaux characteristic of Berkeley can be traced back to such panoramic devices as the Eidophusikon (1781) and to Jeremy Bentham's Penitentiary Panopticon (1791), his architecture of prison surveillance.[5]

It is the problematic and contradictory nature of early Busby Berkeley films such as *Gold Diggers of 1933* that renders them particularly suitable texts for study. Economics and ideology are erased by aesthetics and plot requirements. Similarly, class issues are readily solved when working-class chorus girls marry into the aristocracy. Nevertheless, *Gold Diggers of 1933*, like other Warner Brothers films of the period, did attempt to respond to the social circumstances and worries of Depression America. Its leading artists, Ruby Keeler and Dick Powell, were more down to earth than Paramount's Jeanette MacDonald and Maurice Chevalier, and its songs were lowbrow Broadway show tunes. As the title suggests, the movie's themes include money and the need to make ends meet, examined through the lives of chorus girls. Enduring long hours, anxious to keep a paid job and subject to the commands of men, they provide images of single working women in the 1930s that are not completely mythologized. The major contribution to 1930s' iconography arises from the vision of the show's producer, Barney Hopkins, suitably played by the caustic Ned Sparks. Hopkins wants to see a musical about "men marching—marching in the rain ... doughnuts and crullers—jobs, jobs." His vision is realized in the closing number, "My Forgotten Man," which in a virtuoso sequence conflates soup kitchens, the unemployed and the "Bonus Army" of ex-soldiers, so-called because they marched on Washington in May 1932 to petition for payment of the veterans' bonus. *Gold Diggers of 1933* is framed by themes of the Depression. Early in the film, the rehearsal of "We're in the Money," a song announcing the renewal of prosperity, is ended abruptly and ironically as bailiffs move in to close the theatre.

Despite his imaginative powers and his mastery of cinematic space, Berkeley represented a dead end, since the derivation from Ziegfeld led him too often to reduce his chorus girls to statues on a revolving stage. Throughout his films it is the performance of the camera which is crucial. By contrast, the films of Fred Astaire and Ginger Rogers emphasize dance in front of a restrained camera. Stanley Donen, a central figure in the history of the movie musical, if only for his direction of *Singin' in the Rain* (1952) and *Funny Face* (1957), has drawn attention to Astaire's contribution as a great cinematic innovator. Talking about the impression made on him by Astaire's dance with shadows in *Swing Time* (1936), Donen remarked that:

> ...later Kelly and I did the double exposure thing in *Cover Girl* and the mouse thing in *Anchors Aweigh*, but the spark to me for all that was Fred Astaire, without any question. While he himself literally doesn't know anything about a camera, he knows about movies as something quite different from dancing on the stage. Even the number he did on the stage, the *Top Hat* one, is an unbelievable piece of movie, a sensational idea.[6]

Cinema for Astaire, then, was a means of conveying as fully as possible the nature of his talent and, in the films of the 1930s, that of Ginger Rogers. The words which spring to mind are elegance, confidence, absorption and professionalism. As the dance critic Arlene Croce perceived, in an Astaire-Rogers movie, the only serious business is dancing.[7]

It also assists in the generation of the romance plot, with love, dance and stardom interwoven, notably in *Swing Time*. The beginning of love often coincides with the couple's first dance, and it is through dance that love is recovered. Dance provides an access of energy, a paradigm of liberation, and, of particular importance in the 1930s, a means of exerting control over the body and its existence. The gangster movie genre of the early 1930s proposed an analogous if more violent solution to Depression impotence; significantly several of the hoodlums were played by dancers such as James Cagney and George Raft.

In the Astaire-Rogers movies, the streamlined night club ambience of top hats and silver lamé, of chromium banisters and black glass floors, seems remote from the workaday world of *Gold Diggers of 1933*. *Swing Time* is rather closer, interrogating *Top Hat*'s (1935) glittering parade, mixing the roulette tables of the pre-Depression years with the picket signs of the 1930s. The stars themselves are sites of contradiction. Ginger Rogers on the dance floor is a goddess; yet within the narrative she retains the brashness and edge she displays in the Busby Berkeley movies. Fred Astaire is urbane, dandyish, an aristocrat of the ballroom, yet he is also thin and balding with a tiny voice, a point which Sue Rickard will explore further in her essay in this collection. In *Swing Time* Astaire is Lucky, a dancing gambler/hobo who travels to New York on a freight train. Later in the 1940s and 1950s he would sometimes play more consistently informal roles of the sort often taken by Gene Kelly. The social and economic problems of the Depression may well be displaced by Lucky's choice of love over materialism, yet, in accordance with contemporary populism, the negative characters are rich and the sympathetic ones are relatively poor. Embedded in a milieu pervaded by conspicuous consumption, the plot contrives to present Astaire and Rogers as agents of change, welcoming the thought, as Babington and Evans put it, "of elegant disruption in a world that has become far too fossilised in its conventionality."[8]

Excess and pretension would also find an adversary in the

persona of Gene Kelly, though characteristically mockery was often combined with a certain respect. This ambivalence of attitude could be emphasized by Kelly's own distanciated acting style. While Astaire and Kelly visibly share a continuity on the screen, there is also a difference which Leo Braudy has articulated: "The energy that Astaire defines within a theatrical and socially formal framework Kelly takes outside, into a world somewhat more 'real'."[9] That filmic world is animated by the athleticism, skill and drive of one who is an individual but who also stimulates a group or community and revives the utopian impulse of the musical.

For Gene Kelly himself, the United States of the late 1940s was far from utopian. His liberal opinions almost put him on the Hollywood blacklist. *An American in Paris* (1951) features an artist living in Paris because his work is not acknowledged in America. Kelly himself went to Paris because of the dangers arising from his political views and those of his wife Betsy Blair. Consequently, as Michael Wood has detected, there is an element of strain and apprehension in Kelly's performances as though they anticipated the era of McCarthyism.[10] Indeed, McCarthy's self-destruction at the Army hearings in 1954 is evoked when the gangster boss exposes his own criminal plot on TV in *It's Always Fair Weather* (1955).

Yet to consider the filmic Kelly in an ambience of un-American activities seems to detach him too much from his personae. Many of the characters he assumes are Hollywood icons: the cowboy, the gangster, or Charlie Chaplin, impersonated in the title number from *Singin' in the Rain*. His variegated personae are rooted in the mythology of Norman Rockwell and the *Saturday Evening Post*: Junior Proms, the corner drugstore, hot dogs in the bleachers. The overt atmosphere of those films prior to *It's Always Fair Weather* is one of confidence, success and well-being, already discussed by Carey Wall, which finds a parallel in the popular magazines of the 1940s, *Time* and *Life*. That sense of well-being is ubiquitous, allowing Kelly's basically friendly, small-town nature to become overlaid with a brash aggressive manner appropriate to an overcrowded urban environment, turning Kelly into what Stanley Donen called "the sharp Broadway wise guy."[11]

In *The Hollywood Musical*, Jane Feuer emphasizes the self-reflexive nature of musicals, especially after 1950, which results in parody, nostalgia, and a synthesis of past and present.[12] *Singin' in the Rain* is exemplary in this respect. It debunks theatre, silent movies and early sound films, but it glorifies musical comedy. When the city is celebrated in "Broadway Melody" as the source of entertainment (music, color, dance, neon), the locations are explicitly those of show business: Columbia Burlesque, Palace Vaudeville, Ziegfeld Follies. Other allusions include Busby Berkeley, satirized in the "Beautiful Girl" number, George Raft and his coin-flipping routine in the "Broadway Melody" ballet, and Douglas Fairbanks in swashbuckling scenes reminiscent also of the dream dances in earlier Kelly movies, *Anchors Aweigh* (1945) and *The Pirate* (1948). Leo Braudy remarked that "almost all the dances in the film contain parodies of earlier dances and dancers in the same somewhat mocking homage that characterizes the attitude to Impressionism in *An American in Paris*."[13] Indeed, Kelly's range as a performer enables him at times to adopt the bearing of the silent comedian: slightly bemused by his surroundings but endlessly inventive and, in the title number, making an authentic artistic challenge to that cultural establishment of literature, art and classical music adumbrated in the stage setting.

Although Stanley Donen insisted that *It's Always Fair Weather*, far from being cynical or pessimistic, was sugar-coated, it marked a distinct change in the mood of the movie musical.[14] Critics like Michael Wood came to regard the movie as mirroring a decline in American confidence during the 1950s.[15] The beginning, in which three demobilized soldiers arrive in New York, suggests a rerun of *On the Town* (1949). Indeed, the settings are visibly the same, a New York of taxis, bars, nightclubs, and streets that generate dancing. But the lyricism of the earlier film's opening, in which dawn sunlight bathed the cityscape of New York, is significantly absent. Soon the Cinemascope process is used to separate the ex-soldiers and to create a mood of disillusion and alienation. The three guys become stereotypes, respectively, of the organization man, the suburban father and the "smart guy." By the end of the film, experience in the postwar city has brought the trio a deeper self-knowledge, so that Kelly can sing, albeit with some detachment, "I Like Myself," and the final note is one of an optimism much more muted than in earlier musicals.

During the 1960s and 1970s the musical struggled as its traditional lavishness made it economically impracticable, and as events at home and abroad (Vietnam, race riots, and other cultural and political conflicts) reduced its generic message to irrelevance. Not for the first time, film-makers turned to a disinfected Europe (*The Sound of Music*, 1965), or to turn-of-the-century small-town America (*The Music Man*, 1962). Alternatively, in more than one sense, musicals would document communal events (*Hair*, 1967; *Woodstock*, 1970), producing films in which, as Leo Braudy remarked, the audience becomes the star.[16]

Musicals survived by a mixture of the familiar and the unusual. *On a Clear Day You Can See Forever* (1970) incorporates the search for a paradisal world. Of course, this had often been a feature of earlier musicals; but now there was a significant difference. As Andy Medhurst remarked:

> This world is not, however, the ideal romance of *Top Hat*, the perfect show of *Gold Diggers of 1933*, the mythicised New York of *On the Town*, or even the dream village of *Brigadoon*—it is purely abstract, wholly internalised, a utopian state of mind.[17]

Projecting the actors finally into a cloudy dream world, *On a Clear Day You Can See Forever* participates in the 1960s' fascination with mysticism and the non-rational, with reincarnation and techniques of personal growth. Stylistically, it recoils from big production routines, which are replaced by soliloquies. In the last of these, Daisy, played by Barbra Streisand, celebrates herself in isolation. It is tempting to detect here evidence of the culture of narcissism of the 1970s, or at least of qualities of self-indulgence and egotism attributed to Streisand's stage and screen personality. These characteristics, it is alleged, are discernible in "Don't Rain on my Parade" from *Funny Girl* (1968) and "Let's Hear It For Me" from *Funny Lady* (1975). Such an assumption ignores Streisand's wit and irony evident in the

51

parodic elements of "I'm the Greatest Star" (*Funny Girl*). Indeed, one of Streisand's skills has been the exaggeration of what Susan Sontag has called "corny flamboyant femaleness." This technique, denying essentialism, states that there are only *performances* of femininity. By interrogating femininity and refusing its conventional aspects Streisand, like Bette Midler and Judy Garland before them, has achieved a cult status in the category of cultural taste known as "camp."[18]

From the early films of Busby Berkeley onwards, camp has been available to the musical, its penchant for bad taste best remembered through "Springtime For Hitler," Mel Brooks's notorious Berkeley pastiche in *The Producers* (1967). Nazism as cultural capital belongs more securely to "kitsch," that petit-bourgeois category distinguishable by its artistic pretensions. It was, rather, to the decadence and sexual ambiguities of urban Germany in the immediate pre-Hitler period that Bob Fosse turned for his camp-inflected musical, *Cabaret* (1972). Camp as bad taste is more evident in Fosse's *All That Jazz* (1979), where the homage to Busby Berkeley takes place in an operating theatre; or in the Broadway show *Chicago* (1975), where he attempts to turn Carl Sandburg's "City of the Big Shoulders" into a version of the Weimar Republic.[19] The distance travelled since the 1930s is indicated by camp's opposition to that search for utopian, liberated identities which had been a feature of the musical throughout its history. There are no facile illusions of happiness in *Cabaret*.

Despite Fosse's quasi-Brechtian style, despite the film's X certificate, the first ever given in Britain to a musical, *Cabaret* does exhibit features of the genre. I discussed earlier the tension between reality and escape, the preoccupation with show business, the predilection for quotation, reference, and pastiche. The all-black costumes, hunched body poses and the use of the derby go back to the film of *The Pajama Game* (choreographed by Fosse in 1957). His fragmented style, isolating movement by different parts of the body, can be traced to Afro-American jazz dance, and Eccentric dancers of the 1920s onwards such as Rubberlegs Williams and Earl "Snake Hips" Tucker. In the opening number the audience on film includes a lesbian wielding an impressive cigarette holder, a bloated businessman, and a youth wearing a Nazi armband. The iconographic debt is to the drawings and paintings of George Grosz and Otto Dix, and to the disintegrated society of *Neue Sachlichkeit.* Liza Minnelli is an appropriate centrepiece for Fosse's abrasive, disjointed routines in *Cabaret.* Minnelli is a brash singer, gauche dancer and intense performer, and, like Streisand, she is an ambiguous figure, linked in this musical as much to male as to female sexuality. In her first song, "Mein Herr," Minnelli as cabaret artist recalls Marlene Dietrich and a filmic history of androgyny that includes Minnelli's mother Judy Garland. The whole movie gives the *coup de grâce* to the "organic" musical. In 1980, the film critic David Thomson wrote, "Liza remains as innocent looking and as much a guarantee of upheaval as Louise Brooks' Lulu in *Pandora's Box.*"[20]

The circle is complete. Louise Brooks, one-time Ziegfeld Follies dancer, beat Dietrich for the role of the whore whose amorality exposes a violent, decadent society. *Pandora's Box* (1928) anticipates the Berlin of the Kit-Kat Club, whose frenzy in *Cabaret* is not wholly removed from the Saint Vitus' dance of the USA in the early 1970s, still mired in Vietnam and with a further media entertainment in the wings—Watergate.

NOTES

1 Jane Feuer, "The Self-Reflective Musical and the Myth of Entertainment," in *Genre: The Musical,* ed. Rick Altman (London: Routledge/BFI, 1981), p. 172.

2 Bruce Babington and Peter William Evans, *Blue Skies and Silver Linings: Aspects of the Hollywood Musical* (Manchester: Manchester University Press, 1985), p. 49.

3 See Mikhail M. Bakhtin, *The Dialogic Imagination: Four Essays,* trans. Caryl Emerson and Michael Holquist (Austin: University of Texas Press, 1981).

4 Bruce Norman, *The Inventing of America* (London: BBC, 1976), pp. 196–9.

5 On the Eidophusikon, see Richard D. Altick, *The Shows of London* (Cambridge, MA: The Belknap Press of Harvard University Press, 1978), pp. 121–7. On panoramas generally, see Ralph Hyde, *Panoramania!: The Art and Entertainment of the 'All-Embracing' View* (London: Trefoil Publications, 1988). On Bentham's Panopticon, see Michel Foucault, *Discipline and Punish: The Birth of the Prison* (1977; rpt. Harmondsworth, Middlesex: Penguin, 1979), pp. 200–9. Plate 3 reproduces Bentham's influential plan.

6 "Interview with Stanley Donen," *Movie* 24 (Spring 1977), p. 33.

7 Arlene Croce, *The Fred Astaire & Ginger Rogers Book* (New York: Vintage Books, 1977), pp. 6–7.

8 Babington and Evans, p. 99.

9 Leo Braudy, *The World in a Frame: What We See in Films* (Garden City, NY: Anchor, 1977), p. 148.

10 Michael Wood, *America in the Movies* (London: Secker & Warburg, 1975), p. 164.

11 Donen, *Movie* 24, p. 27.

12 Jane Feuer, *The Hollywood Musical* (London: BFI/Macmillan, 1982) pp. 102–6.

13 Braudy, p. 154.

14 Donen, *Movie* 24, p. 34.
15 Wood, pp. 158–64.
16 Braudy, p. 170.
17 Andy Medhurst, "The Musical," *The Cinema Book*, ed. Pam Cook (London: BFI, 1985), p. 112.
18 See Susan Sontag, "Notes on 'Camp'," and "The 'Salmagundi' Interview," *A Susan Sontag Reader* (Harmondsworth, Middlesex: Penguin, 1983), pp. 109, 338.
19 Carl Sandburg, "Chicago," *The New Oxford Book of American Verse*, ed. Richard Ellmann (New York: Oxford University Press, 1976), p. 422.
20 David Thomson, *A Biographical Dictionary of the Cinema* (London: Secker and Warburg, 1980), p. 413.

5

Holy Yumpin' Yiminy: Scandinavian Immigrant Stereotypes in the Early Twentieth Century American Musical

Anne-Charlotte Hanes Harvey

Mainstream America appears to define itself in opposition to immigrants, the often unskilled, poor and supplicant. The latest group to arrive and struggle with the new language and culture is also made the butt of the same generic "ethnic" jokes applied to its predecessor, the term "ethnic" implying the existence of a dominant, non-ethnic culture. If the musical reflects American culture and history, one would expect it to feature a succession of ethnic types, introduced on stage in the order in which the various groups appeared on the American scene: the Blacks, the French, the Irish, the Germans, the Chinese, the Norwegians, the Swedes, the Danes, the Finns, the Jews, the Italians, the Poles, the Puerto-Ricans, the Mexicans, the Latin Americans, the Vietnamese. Yet only to an extent is this true. All ethnic groups did not end up as characters on stage, and the appearance of those who did was far from predictable.

Long considered unsuitable for serious research, and still paradoxically politically suspect, the comparative study of ethnic stereotypes remains a largely unexplored field. Ethnic stage types are better documented, particularly types representing prominent immigrant groups like the Irish, though the emphasis tends to be on the biography of the performer creating the character rather than on analysis of the character itself.[1] The study of the ethnic character on the musical stage is largely neglected. This is regrettable, since it was the popular music theater, along with vaudeville, that was particularly instrumental in promoting the ethnic stereotypes which have survived, with variations, to this day.

The study of ethnic types on the musical stage can reveal as much about the musical and its audience as about the portrayal of a particular ethnic group. The fundamental question is one of function, and to understand the function of the ethnic character in the musical better, it is instructive to look at one particular ethnic group and its representation on the musical stage. This essay will focus on the Scandinavians and how they were portrayed and stereotyped in American popular entertainment during the two formative decades from 1900 to 1920.

Migration from Scandinavia to America began in the second quarter of the nineteenth century, peaked in the 1870s and 1880s, and ended with the Depression. Yet the Scandinavian stereotype did not appear on the stage until the 1890s, played its major role in the first two decades of the century, and then faded but never quite disappeared.[2] Why does such a time lag occur? The reasons are threefold. First, there has to be sufficient psychological distance from their first arrival for the immigrant characters to be indisputably comic.[3] Second, it takes time for an ethnic group to become numerous enough to be stereotyped. Third, for a type to be commercially viable, it has to be instantly recognizable. In short, the ethnic group had to reach a certain critical mass and be distinctive enough to be profitably parodied. In comparison with other ethnic groups (for instance, Blacks, Irish, French, Germans, or Jews), the Scandinavians constituted a relatively small immigrant population with less visibility in the entertainment business centres of New York and Chicago. The larger number of Irish cops than Swedish lumberjacks on the American musical stage reflects, among other things, the fact that there have always been many more Irish policemen than Swedish loggers in New York City.

Scandinavia is the collective term for Norway, Denmark, and Sweden.[4] Notwithstanding occasional pan-Scandinavian strivings, when immigrant entertainers and songwriters from any one of the Scandinavian countries created "ethnic" characters, these tended to be highly origin-specific, intensely Norwegian or Danish or Swedish. In contrast, American popular musicians and librettists did not distinguish between the three countries and created a generic Scandinavian (later parodically known as "Skandehuuvian") type. A closer look at the Scandinavian type reveals a predominantly Swedish component (not surprisingly, since Sweden contributed more immigrants than Norway or Denmark) with some Norwegian traits added. In early popular entertainment, the term "Scandinavian" was often used inter-changeably with "Swedish." To this day, American actors studying stage accents and dialects will find textbooks that teach a generic Scandinavian accent which does not exist outside of the stage.[5]

What were the Scandinavian types like? A 1918 Tin Pan Alley song called "Holy Yumpin' Yiminy" gives us a good idea.[6] In this song, the Swedish immigrant girl Hilda rhapsodizes about her boyfriend Yonnie Yonson who also hails from Sweden and who "seems to know 'bout cows and dogs and everything." She describes him as "slow" and "yust as clumsy as can be" and con-tinues to admit that "he no ban much on reading books, and he ban worse when it comes to looks," but those negative traits pale when Hilda thinks of "how my Yonnie can love!" Hilda's lyrics here exhibit two typical modifications of standard English ascribed to the Swedish immigrant: the substitution of [y] for [j], and the use of "ban" as a mispronounced version, to be used in all tenses and cases, of the verb "to be." While Yonnie is described in the song, Hilda is depicted on the cover of the sheet music. She is pigeon-toed, wears a gingham-check dress, long blond hair braided in two flipped-up pigtails, and a self-con-sciously cute expression, including huge dimples. Of course, Hilda also unwittingly characterizes herself by her breathless response to Yonnie and his lovemaking.

"Holy Yumpin' Yiminy" was just one of many Scandinavian dialect songs flourishing from around the turn of the century and still to be heard in the Upper Midwest states. They include such favourites as "Swanson, Swensen, and Jensen" and "I Ban Swede From North Dakota." Hilda Honson and Yonnie Yonson are well-developed examples of two Scandinavian stereotypes that survive, together with their descendants, to this day. They appear, for instance, in a 1917 song, "Hello Wisconsin," which both Emma Cook and "red hot mama" Sophie Tucker helped launch. In the 1930s there was a brief renaissance for singing Scandinavian ethnic characters with the Chicago radioshow "Sentimental Selma," featuring a Swedish maid advertising Wyler's bouillon cubes over the Chicago airwaves.[7] In the 1940s and 1950s Harry Stewart made a career as the Scandinavian dialect comedian Yogi Yorgesson. Stan Boreson is still to be heard in the Pacific Northwest with songs like "Blue Goose Snoose." (The Scandinavian male immigrant is strongly identified with this form of tobacco—hence the nickname "Snoose Boulevard" for the main street in Swedish-American neighbourhoods.) Older American television audiences may remember Inger Stevens' farmer's daughter, and Virginia Stevens's Mrs Olsen with her "mountain grown coffee." Yet another, more recent, television personality is the Swedish Chef on the Muppet Show. But most recognizable is Yonnie, the slow, honest, naive Scandinavian farm laborer or lumberjack, passionate only when it comes to ethnic delicacies, his girlfriend and justice, in that order.

Where did they come from, Yonnie and Hilda? When and how did they appear on the American scene? The prototypes of Yonnie on the English-speaking American stage were probably the eponymous characters in the dialect comedies *Ole Olsen* (1889) and the hugely successful *Yon Yonson* (1890) by Augustus "Gus" Heege.[8] The script of *Ole Olsen* has not survived. That of *Yon Yonson* has, and its plot seems silly and contrived today. The action is set in the woods of northern Minnesota where Yon, a Swedish lumberjack, manages to save his fellow travellers from a con-artist. One of the ladies in the party turns out to be his long-lost sister, while another loses her heart to him. Appropriately, a surprise discovery of a legacy gives Yon a fortune and a prominent position in society. The play toured widely, and was on the road as late as 1917. *Ole Olsen* and *Yon Yonson* were soon followed by similar plays, such as *Hans Hanson* (1898) and *Yenuine Yentleman* (1895). No doubt their popularity owed a lot to the stereotyped leading character. Yon wears big boots, a checked vest, a long scarf, and a cloth cap pushed back on his head. His hair is a prominent feature, yellow and rather unruly. In all illustrations it has the appearance of a wig that is supposed to look like a wig.[9] He is now inextricably linked with the familiar cyclical song, "My name is Yon Yonson, I come from Wisconsin, I work in the lumber mill there..."—which describes his character exactly. The female prototype probably appeared a little later on the stage, in the character of Lena Anderson in *That Little Swede* (1904). Judging from a publicity photograph of 1905, she carries a carpet bag, wears a mismatched dress, jacket and hat, and is short-necked and pigeon-toed.[10]

On the musical stage, the heyday for the Scandinavian character came roughly between 1900 and 1920. The peak year was 1904, with no less than three major New York musical productions featuring Scandinavian characters: *The Forbidden Land*, *Eric of Sweden*, and *It Happened in Nordland*, which had music composed by Victor Herbert. *The Forbidden Land* places the stereotype in an unusual context. Its subtitle is "A Tibetan Comic Opera," possibly representing a parodic response to the string of popular "oriental" shows beginning with *The Mikado* (1885) and continuing with *Pearl of Pekin* (1888), *A Trip to Chinatown* (1890), *The Geisha* (1896) and *A Chinese Honeymoon* (1902). The other two Scandinavian musicals have more conventional romantic plots, as their names suggest.

The cavalcade of Scandinavian characters on the musical stage continued in single songs, mostly produced and published in Tin Pan Alley. The popular music scene in the two first decades of the century was complex, in part because of its explosive growth and intensely commercial nature. There was only a limited distinction between songs written separately and those written as part of a musical. Because of star pressure and commercial interests, popular songs were continually interpolated into musicals, which sometimes were no more than a framework for a series of unrelated but best-selling songs. Indeed, interpolation was so common a practice with successful songs that, as late as 1960, the only two composers to have made their debut on the New York stage with complete musical scores were Rudolf Friml and Leonard Bernstein.[11] George Gershwin is typical in beginning his stage career by means of a single song interpolated into an existing show.

"Scandinavian" songs were therefore performed by dialect singers or comedians in many different venues and contexts. An instance from 1909 is "Christina Swanson," which first appeared as an "illustrated" song, one performed, that is, with accompanying slides in nickelodeons. The illustrated song was a relatively shortlived phenomenon between vaudeville and film, conceived as a commercial gimmick by music publishers. "Christina Swanson" was popular, and so it reappeared later in 1909 as an interpolation in the musical *The Old Town*. Published sheet-music for *The Old Town* indicates that at least three different composer-lyricist teams contributed to the show.[12]

Looking at the gallery of Scandinavian characters in these musicals and songs, we find two basic approaches. One approach, related to the tradition of operetta, gives us a romanticized picture of stately people in a Cold Old Country. Sometimes, as in *Eric of Sweden* and *It Happened in Nordland*, the picture becomes detached from any recognizable "reality." The only reason, it would seem, for referring to Sweden at all is that it is regarded as an exotic place, and rhymes with Eden. "Fair Land Sweden," from *Eric of Sweden*, and "I've a Garden in Sweden," from *Little Miss Fix-It* (1911), both use this rhyme. It follows from the distant and exotic setting that no spectre of emigration hangs over the inhabitants.[13]

The other approach gives us the Scandinavian as an immigrant in an American, often Midwestern, setting. These characters are based, however loosely and no matter how caricatured, on some kind of direct observation, including that of immigrant speech. This is where Yonnie and his Hilda in "Holy Yumpin' Yiminy" belong. Here, too, is to be found Hilda Honson, who is trying to reach her particular Yonnie Yonson by telephone in "Hello Wisconsin." This is where we find Christina Swanson, the nasty golddigger who rejects her "lumberyack" Yonnie after he has spent all his money on her. Such social "realism" even informs the "Tibetan Comic Opera," *The Forbidden Land*. Although the action is set in Lhasa, where Hulda the Swedish maid has accompanied her American mistress, Hulda portrays the stereotypical immigrant, singing and yodelling "Ay Vant to

Go Back to Sveden." It is probably no coincidence that *Yon Yonson* and *The Forbidden Land* were first produced in the Upper Midwest, while *Eric of Sweden* and *It Happened in Nordland* appeared in New York.

It will by now have become obvious that the typical male Scandinavian is almost always called Yon, or Yonnie/Yohnnie, or Ole. If he has a surname, it is Yonson/Yohnson or Olson/Olsen. A somewhat later type is Sven or Swan, with the surname of—what else?—Swanson. Yonnie (Ole, Sven) is big and strong—in "Hello Wisconsin" he is "over six feet high"— and not much when it comes to looks, as we found out in "Holy Yumpin' Yiminy." He does not read books, but seems to have enough sense to run a farm, and to leave a girl who is bleeding him dry. He works with his hands, overwhelmingly as a farm-hand or lumberjack or gardener. His occupations, and many of the songs, place him firmly in the Upper Midwest. He is faithful and loyal, once he has made up his mind. In some ways he resembles Jonathan, the American Yankee prototype that can be traced back to Royall Tyler's *The Contrast* (1787), in his sus-picion of all sophistication and refinement, which here trans-lates into disdain for anything outside Minnesota. True to his (transplanted) roots, he professes:

> Ay cannot see New York at all
> ven I recall St. Paul,
> an' as for Europe, to tell the truth,
> it's miles behind Duluth.[14]

Pronounced with a Scandinavian accent, the [th] in Duluth (and "truth") becomes a [t], perhaps one of the reasons why Duluth figures prominently as a comic place in popular entertainment at this time. This no doubt accounts for the title of the musical, *The Duke from Duluth* (1905), which was intended as a parodic echo of *The Prince of Pilsen* (1903), a highly successful musical which also inspired such take-offs as *The Duchess of Dantzic* (1905) and *The Earl of Pawtucket* (1903). Duluth also appears in the song "Two To Duluth," from the musical *The Heart Breakers* (1911), in which the request for two tickets is misheard as "Too-too-de-loot."[15] Yonnie is also gullible and an easy mark for smarter men or women. He likes to take a drink but, curiously,

61

he does not use "snoose." As far as his sex appeal goes, while Hilda gets the shivers just thinking of him, he cannot control a golddigger because he is "crazy like a mule" and "looks like a yoke."[16]

Yonnie's female counterpart is a little more complex. In her "good" manifestation, she is most often called Hilda or Hulda, sometimes Tilly (*Tilly Olson*, 1903) or Lena (*That Little Swede*). Like the majority of Swedish female immigrants, she is a domestic servant, dairy maid, or farmer's wife.[17] Just like Yonnie, she is practical and faithful and hardworking. She is not misled by appearances and ignores Yonnie's lack of sophistication and looks. Hilda is usually cheerful and quick, in contrast to Yonnie with his doleful countenance and deliberate tempo. She has more savvy, is more adaptable and more easily assimilated than he. This, too, agrees with demographic data about Swedish immigrants. With time, Hilda (Hulda) becomes Selma (Thelma) or Lena, living on as a Swedish cook in numerous dialect monologues and jokes.

There is also a "bad" manifestation of the Scandinavian female. Her name is never Hilda or Hulda and she is, but for her name and her accent, indistinguishable from such other American female archetypes as the vamp and the gangster moll. Christina Swanson of 1909 is joined in the 1930s and 1940s by Olga ("I Ban Swede from North Dakota") who seduces the naive North Dakotan farmhand in a bar in Minneapolis, and the thoroughly bad girls Hanna, Nanna, and Lanna, who slip their unsuspecting victim a Mickey Finn (in "Swanson, Swensen, and Jensen"). There is also a third female type, the married immigrant woman in an urban setting. Developed by the Norwegian-American sisters Ethel and Eleonora Olson, this type is characterized by intense family loyalty, patriotism, and delight in middle-class (sub)urban life. The sisters wrote their own Norwegian-accent monologues and were uniquely successful, touring, often on the Chatauqua circuit, between 1905 and 1925.[18] The sisters' creation is a precurser of Mama in John van Druten's 1944 play *I Remember Mama*, turned into a musical by Richard Rodgers in 1959.

The general temperament and occupations of Yonnie and Hilda, Sven and Selma may have been based on observable reality, but the blurring of distinctions between Scandinavian countries in the mind of the general public was increased by the musical form. Only an impression of generic exoticism or rusticity was desired, and the merest shorthand that would achieve this impression was used. The cover of "Hello Wisconsin" shows a girl in Dutch costume. The accent in "Minnesota" (*The Old Town*) and "Ay Vant to Go Back to Sveden" (*The Forbidden Land*) comes close to German, changing "with" to the German "mit" instead of the Swedish "med" or the Swedish-American "vid." In *The Forbidden Land* one hears a Slavic echo in the reference to "Svensky land." Musically, there is very little that can be considered Scandinavian beyond general sprightliness and the waltz rhythms in "Ay Vant to Go Back to Sveden" and "Minnesota." "Sentimental Selma" is an authentic schottische (the composer was Norwegian), but the gypsy call "hi, hi" in "Scandinavia" (1921) has a distinctly non-Scandinavian flavour.[19]

A puzzling phenomenon is the yodelling which crops up in several places. In *The Forbidden Land*, Hulda's chorus is a yodel, and in the same year there is a yodel in "Northland Lullaby" from *Eric of Sweden*. A 1908 advertisement in the Swedish-American newspaper *Rockfords-posten* for an upcoming performance of *Yon Yonson* announces that the songs in the play will include "the old familiar yodeling."[20] Yodelling is not a Scandinavian art. In Sweden, yodelling is considered distinctly Swiss or Austrian. Possibly the confusion between Sweden and Switzerland already existed at the turn of the century, or perhaps the star of the show, Ben Hendricks, single-handedly created this musical stereotype. Hendricks, it seems, was an accomplished yodeller, first including a yodel in the "Northland Lullaby" he composed for himself to sing in the 1904 *Eric of Sweden*. This apparently inspired Victor Herbert to give Hulda a yodel, too, and Hendricks then interpolated the "Lullaby" four years later in his performance in *Yon Yonson*.[21]

The changes of name from Yonnie to Sven and Hilda to Selma suggest a development in the Scandinavian types. They become more generic, more non-specific, more Americanized. Their "ethnicity" eventually hinges on a single trait (slowness) or expression ("yah sure," "yu bat") or mispronunciation (the substitution of [y] for [j]). Sometimes their ethnic background is suggested by nothing more than their name. In Ray Perkins' 1921 hit "Scandinavia," sung by Eddie Cantor, there is nothing that is Swedish about Yonnie but his name. He dreams, not of lutefisk and peasoup, but of chocolate cake and apple pie. His "Swedish" girlfriend, most unusually in a decade of proliferating Swedish chefs, cannot even cook:

> You know for you I would die,
> but never ask me to try
> those Swedish pastry of yours,
> excuse me, because
> I really don't think I want to die now...

More typical is the 1935 "Sentimental Selma," who *can* cook, is favourably compared with Greta Garbo, and "goes to Hollywood."[22]

Why was it the Scandinavian that became the rustic yokel par excellence and not some other farming immigrant group, for example the Irish? I would suggest that this adoption was the result of several conditions being met. The immigrant yokel had to come from a strong rural tradition; he had to appear slow and therefore could not (like the Irish) speak fluent English; and he had to have a placid northern European temper, being physically powerful and clumsy rather than lithe and dexterous. I would also suggest that in the creation of the immigrant yokel type, the Scandinavians' own stereotypical image of themselves gradually filtered into the American consciousness and resulted in the types we recognize even today.

Popular entertainment among the Scandinavian immigrants, especially the Swedes, was not sophisticated. Just as in the Old Country, comic songs and monologues performed by a *bond-komiker* (a "peasant comedian" or rustic comic) were very popular. The *bondkomiker* assumed the persona of a wide-eyed rustic, slow, easily fooled, naive and goodhearted. The comedy derived from his provincial speech, his general lack of sophistication, and especially his bewilderment in the face of urban, "modern" life. Swedish-American theater was modelled on popular entertainment back in Sweden, and consisted of a main diet of farces of German or French origin, some national romantic dramas, a sprinkling of serious modern plays, and a good deal of folk plays.[23] The best loved of all plays in Swedish-America was *Värmlänningarna* (*The People of Värmland*), a six-act folk play with music and dancing. Written in Sweden in 1846, it was first performed in the United States in Chicago in 1884 and remained a staple in Swedish-American theatre into the 1950s.[24] The play is set on an estate in Värmland in the early 1800s. Among its gallery of rural types is Löpar-Nisse, a *bondkomik* prototype and a touchstone role for comic actors, amateur or professional, in Sweden and Swedish-America. As late as 1928–29, Swedish-America's only professional entertainer Hjalmar Petterson, better known under his *bondkomiker* stagename of Olle i Skratthult, toured the United States with a production of *Värmlänningarna*, in which he played Löpar-Nisse.

To what extent did the *bondkomik* types from Swedish-American ethnic theater touch and influence mainstream American entertainment? There appears to have been more contact between the two than has previously been assumed, particularly when one remembers that, before the turn of the century, there already existed a second-generation, English-speaking immigrant audience partaking of and contributing to ethnic as well as mainstream culture. Some instances of direct contact are documented. Gus Heege, the author of *Yon Yonson*, was second-generation half-Swedish, half-German. A number of singers and actors of Scandinavian descent performed both in their own ethnic theater and on the mainstream stage. One example is the singer Arthur Donaldson, who scored a great success in the title roles of *The Prince of Pilsen* and *Yon Yonson*, but who was also popular in Chicago's Swedish theater, singing leading roles from Gilbert and Sullivan, in Swedish. He was even given leave of absence on each Sunday his road-company played in Chicago, so that he could perform with the Swedish theatre in the afternoon.[25] Another, later, example is Olle i Skratthult, who came to the United States in 1906 and toured with Swedish *bondkomik* material for over two decades. For many years he appeared at the Minnesota State Fair, where his all-Swedish shows were great hits with general American audiences. It is reported that a local tribe of Ojibway Indians never missed an opportunity to see Olle perform; indeed, a photo-

65

graph exists showing Olle and his troupe outside his tent with two Ojibway.[26] When Olle produced *Värmlänningarna* in Boston in 1928, its famous Symphony Orchestra played for his Swedish company. Swedish comedian Charles Widdeen and the Norwegian-American Olson sisters were among singers and monologists who changed their performances to English for the benefit of second-generation immigrant audiences, and recorded material in English as well as their native tongue.

The question of overlap of the mainstream and ethnic stages is far from simple. A comparison between the Irish-American and Swedish-American theaters is instructive. Both theaters feature the "greenhorn," the recent immigrant, as a comic character.[27] They differ in that the Irish stage character was accessible to mainstream audiences from the beginning, while the point at which the Swedish character becomes a potential contributor is, of course, when the performance is done in English. In the Irish-American theater, it is hard therefore to say which types were created for internal use, and which were for mainstream consumption. In the Swedish-American theater, on the other hand, the Swedish-created rustic type appears to have entered the mainstream in the 1890s with Heege's "Yon Yonson" plays that toured the country well into the twentieth century.

Whether or not the American stereotype of the typical Scandinavian was influenced by the imported *bondkomik* characters, the types are very similar in appearance and function. Born out of the clash between the old rural way of life and the new urban, industrialized one in late nineteenth-century Scandinavia, the type served to alleviate the underlying anxiety about being propelled into the machine age. The yokel was so ignorant that anyone could feel superior to him and laugh at his attempts to cope with, for instance, a telephone or motorcycle. The new century's infatuation with the machine is reflected in numerous songs about aeroplanes, automobiles, and speedy means of transportation. Bafflement in the face of the machine became a trademark of the rustic yokel character. The theme was explored by the Olson sisters in a comic monologue about a Norwegian woman using the telephone for the first time. It appeared, too, in Swedish *bondkomik* songs and was promptly imported into America by Olle i Skratthult. One of his great hits was "Motorcykeln" (the Motor Cycle). In this song the rustic buys a motorbike and sidecar. As soon as it runs out of petrol, he hitches his horse to it and uses it as a buggy.

America presented an aggravated example of bafflement in the face of the machine. In America, Scandinavians had to cope with a move not only from a rural to an urban environment, but also from a Swedish farm to an American city. The yokel becomes a greenhorn and is recast accordingly. He is portrayed as speaking broken English, making comic mistakes and substitutions. Mixed-language comedy is a fleeting genre, enjoyable only to the generation understanding both languages. The enjoyment derives largely from a sense of superiority over greenhorns who are portrayed as "those poor slobs who can't even speak right." It was, of course, a common phenomenon, and immigrant yokel characters are found in songs, stories, and plays of many ethnic groups besides the Scandinavian.[28]

The Scandinavian stereotype serves much the same function in American popular entertainment. He is recognized by appearance and speech as foreign and simple. His language is characterized primarily by its inflection and melody. Indeed, the speech of the Muppet Swedish Chef has no verbal content, only inflection! The stereotype is rural and reassuringly uncomplicated. He represents the urbanite's "country cousin," the simpler values in life that may have been left behind. In fact, the urbanite's laughter may include elements of yearning for "the good old days," and may be exorcizing the ghost of his own nostalgia. Yonnie and Hilda help reconcile twentieth-century America to an undeniable present and inescapable future.

How did the Scandinavian immigrants respond to the Scandinavian stereotypes foisted on them by popular entertainment, jokes, and cartoons? Compared with some other immigrant groups, the Scandinavians appear on the whole to have taken it all in their stride. Apparently, no one objected to the Yon Yonson persona, perhaps because his underlying characteristics were honesty, fairness, kindness, and integrity. There was, however, some protest against the Swedish dairy-maid Tilly in *Tilly Olson*, who was described by one incensed reviewer as "half crazy."[29] In the large scheme of things, the Scandinavians constituted a small ingredient in the "melting pot," without the numbers or political influence of, say, the Irish or the Italians. For instance, in 1908, Sicilian immigrants in Rochester, struggling to rid themselves of a Mafia stereotype, put on a huge pageant about the life of Jesus, but to little avail. The Irish were more successful. The United Irish Societies hounded the Russell Brothers, an Irish dialect team, for stereotyping Irish women in their vaudeville routine "The Irish Servant Girls." Changing the name of the routine apparently did not satisfy. It is recorded that on one occasion in 1907, in order to avoid the wrath of the Irish, the brothers even performed the routine with a Swedish accent.[30] It was safe to pick on the Swedes. They were not numerous, vociferous, or powerful enough to complain.

The Scandinavian immigrant appeared on the "legitimate" stage before appearing in the musical. In the latter the stereotype is, in a sense, twice removed from the real-life model. If there are two kinds of stereotype, one derived from contemporary, observable models, the other existing by strength of tradition and wide acceptance, the Scandinavian in early twentieth-century musicals is of the second kind. No immigrant, not even one just coming off the gangplank at Ellis Island, looked like Hilda and Yonnie; in fact, no immigrant from Scandinavia had looked anything like them since about 1860. As commercial artists for mass audiences, American popular songwriters were not innovative but rather drew on, perpetuated, and elaborated already-established Scandinavian stereotypes. The "Nordic-setting" characters on the musical stage were more generically heroic or sentimental than Scandinavian. Noble, handsome, blue-eyed, blond, reserved and devoid of a sense of humor, they served as romantic leads. The "American-setting" immigrant characters were common folk of rural origin, trusting, naive, plain and clumsy, sometimes tongue-tied, sometimes talkative, but always mangling the English language. They were the eccentrics, providing comic relief in minor roles, as sidekicks or comic secondary leads. Their songs were billed as "novelties." Yonnie and Hilda summed up and labelled an entire ethnic group for easy handling (or, to use a modern term, "othering") by the average American, although, as we have seen, they represented an artificially-created conglomerate of at least three distinct ethnic groups. In addition, Yonnie and Hilda helped immigrant audience members from the Scandinavian countries exorcize ghosts from their own not-so-distant past, and empowered recent immigrants to cope by laughter with the bewildering present.

Scandinavian stereotypes on the musical stage are clearly not central to the history of the American musical. Yet they are worth looking at for what they reveal about the musical, as well as about ethnic stereotyping. The early twentieth century was a time of high commercial stakes in the business of mass entertainment, tremendous flux in the musical form, proliferation of venues and types of entertainment, and fluid boundaries between genres. Entertainment for the masses was characterized by a restless search for escape, change, color and comedy. Ethnic locales, characters and novelty songs could provide it all. The Scandinavian stereotype was ideal: harmless and innocent, politically safe, socially and intellectually inferior to just about anybody, but also foreign and colorful enough to be exotic. Once launched on the musical stage, Hilda and Yonnie could always be relied on for simple comic relief, appearing sporadically in popular songs down the decades. Is it pure chance that the so-called "loss of American innocence" with American entry into World War I coincided with the appearance of the simplest, sweetest, and most innocent of their manifestations, the 1917 "Hello Wisconsin" and the 1918 "Holy Yumpin' Yiminy"?

NOTES

1   An exception is Douglas Gilbert, *American Vaudeville, Its Life and Times* (New York: Dover, 1940), which describes the ethnic types as well as the performers. A useful survey is given by Carl Wittke, "The Immigrant Theme on the American Stage," *Mississippi Valley Historical Review* 34 (1953), pp. 211–32. I would like to thank Landis K. Magnuson, St. Anselm College, and Douglas McDermott, California State University at Stanislaus, who have undertaken significant research on early Scandinavian dialect plays in the United States, and who have contributed generously to my own, continuing, work on the function of ethnic types in theater.

2   American dramas with non-immigrant Scandinavian characters appeared earlier, in historical tragedies like *Mathilda of Denmark* (1870), *Romer, King of Norway* (1885), and *The Viking* (1888). In the 1880s an occasional contemporary character from Scandinavia cropped up, but there was nothing approaching a recognizable stereotype on the "legitimate" stage until O'Neill's *Anna Christie* (1925).

3   A distinction should be made here, between the reception of the immigrant types by the mainstream "American" culture, and by the growing immigrant population itself. The

meainstream may have thought the immigrants appeared "funny" from the moment they first landed; the immigrants' fellow-countrymen not until later, when they were sufficiently distanced from their own greenhorn days.

4　Sometimes Scandinavia is incorrectly used to refer also to the Nordic countries, thereby also including Finland, Iceland, and the Faeroe Islands.

5　See, for instance, Lewis Hermann and Marguerite Shalett Hermann, *Foreign Dialects* (New York: Theater Arts Books, 1943), p. 316.

6　Bernie Grossman, Nat Vincent and Ed Morton, "Holy Yumpin' Yiminy (How My Yonnie Can Love)" (New York: Joe Morris Music Co., 1918).

7　Harry Ruby, Bert Kalmar and Edgar Leslie, "Hello Wisconsin (Won't You Find My Yonnie Yonson)" (New York: Kalmar, Puck, and Abrahams Consolidated Music Publishers, 1917). Stanford R. Espedal, "Sentimental Selma" (Chicago: Stanford R. Espedal, 1935).

8　Augustus "Gus" Heege, *Yon Yonson*, unpublished, n.d. [1890]. On the first New York production of *Yon Yonson* (in 1891) see *The Best Plays of 1894–99*, ed. John Chapman and Garrison P. Sherwood (New York: Dodd, Mead & Co., 1955), p. 96.

9　Yon's appearance can be seen in stock illustrations and promotional photographs in the Swedish-American press, such as *Rockfords-posten* (Rockford, Ill.), 16 September 1904.

10　*Rockfords-posten*, 9 September 1904 (when Lena's last name is given in the Norwegian form of Anders*en*) and 11 August 1905 (when it is the Swedish Anders*on*).

11　Lehman Engel, *The American Musical Theater* (New York: Macmillan, 1975), p. 22.

12　Terry Sherman, with lyrics by Bob Adams, "Good-bye Christina Swanson," *The Old Town* (New York: Chas. K. Harris, 1909). The three teams are Sherman-Adams, Robyn-Railey, and Luders-Adey.

13　Ben Hendricks, "Fair Land of Sweden," *Eric of Sweden* (New York: The Ellis Music Co., 1904). Murphy, Owens, and Lipton, "I've a Garden in Sweden," *Little Miss Fix-It* by W. J. Hurlbut and Harry B. Smith (American version by [Nora] Bayes and [Jack] Norworth, New York: Norworth Publishing Co., 1911).

14　Alfred G. Robyn, with lyrics by Thomas T. Railey, "Minnesota," from *The Old Town* (New York: M. Witmark & Sons, 1910), p. 5.

15　Gideon Melville, "Two to Duluth," *The Heart Breakers* (New York: M. Witmark and Sons, 1911).

16　Sherman and Adams, "Good-bye Christina Swanson," *The Old Town*.

17　The Scandinavian domestic servant is discussed in Odd S. Lovoll, *A Century of Urban Life* (Champaign: University of Illinois Press, 1988); Joy K. Lintelman, "On My Own: Single, Swedish, and Female in Turn-of-the-Century Chicago," *Cultural and Urban Aspects of an Immigrant People, 1850–1930*, ed. Philip J. Anderson and Dag Blanck (Champaign: University of Illinois Press, 1992); Lintelman, "'America is the Woman's Promised Land': Swedish Immigrant Women and American Domestic Service," *Journal of American Economic History* 8 (1989), pp. 9-23; and Ulf Beijbom, "Pigornas förlovade land," *Svenskamerikanskt* (Växjö: Emigrantinstitutets Vänner, 1990), pp. 99-136.

18　Ethel and Eleonora Olson, *Yust for Fun* (1925; rpt. ed. Paul F. Anderson, Minneapolis: Eggs Press, 1979).

19　Frederic Chapin, "Ay Vant to Go Back to Sveden," *The Forbidden Land: A Comic Opera*, book and lyrics by Guy F. Steely (New York: M. Witmark & Sons, 1904). Ray Perkins, "Scandinavia: Sing Dose Song and Make Dose Music," *Midnight Rounders* (New York: Stark and Cowan, 1921).

20　*Rockfords-posten*, 6 November 1908.

21　This supposition is strengthened by the fact that "What It Means," another song from *Eric of Sweden*, is also mentioned in the *Yon Yonson* advertisement. In addition, the musical's "A Swagger Swedish Swell" may well be the same as "A Bane a Swell" from *Yon Yonson*.

22　Perkins, "Scandinavia: Sing Dose Song and Make Dose Music," *Midnight Rounders*. Espedal, "Sentimental Selma."

23　The most extensive study of Swedish theater in America is Henriette K. Naeseth, *Swedish Theater of Chicago 1868–1950* (Rock Island, Ill.: Augustana Historical Soc., 1951). Two briefer and more recent treatments are Anne-Charlotte Harvey, "Swedish-

American Theater," *Ethnic Theater in the United States*, ed. Maxine Schwartz Seller (Westport, CT: Greenwood Press, 1983), pp. 491–524; and Lars Furuland, "Från *Värmländingarne* till *Slavarna på Molokstorp*," *Ljus över landet* (Uppsala: Gidlunds, 1991), pp. 236–60.

24 Naeseth, *Swedish Theater of Chicago*, p. 284.

25 Naeseth, *Swedish Theater of Chicago*, p. 369.

26 Photograph, Olle i Skratthult Museum, Munkfors, Värmland, Sweden. The woman member of Skratthult's team is seen wearing what was no doubt felt to be a quintessentially Swedish costume, but is Lapp. For more information on Skratthult, see Maury Bernstein, "Olle i Skratthult and Scandinavian-American Vaudeville," *American Popular Music*, ed. Johannes Riedel (Minneapolis: University of Minnesota Press, 1976); and Harvey, "Swedish-American Theater."

27 Maureen Murphy, "Irish-American Theater," *Ethnic Theater in the United States*, ed. Seller, pp. 221–36.

28 Maxine Schwartz Seller, "Introduction," *Ethnic Theater in the United States*, ed. Seller, p. 8.

29 *Rockfords-posten*, 26 August 1904.

30 Seller, "Introduction," *Ethnic Theater in the United States*, ed. Seller, pp. 10–11. Geraldine Maschio, "Ethnic Knockabout Comedy: The Career of the Russell Brothers," Paper delivered at the American Theater Association Convention, New York City, 1986, p. 7.

6

Movies in Disguise: Negotiating Censorship and Patriarchy Through the Dances of Fred Astaire and Ginger Rogers

Sue Rickard

The Hollywood musical has always had the potential for various kinds of double-life, in both its presentation and consumption. The musical, like much Hollywood film, expresses and penetrates both the public and private areas of human experience. Superficially it appears to show images as a kind of filmed reality, but the form in which these images are presented can act powerfully on the imagination to encourage a much deeper and more personal interpretation from individual spectators, and nowhere more powerfully than in the sexual arena. Despite efforts made in the early decades of the century to rid cinemas of their nickelodeon peep-show reputation, the experience of going to the movies had always retained an atmosphere of sexual potential. For young people particularly, not only could they learn techniques of love-making from their screen heroes and heroines, but the cinema was a place where some of those lessons might be put into immediate practice. Movie-houses were places of public entertainment, yet the darkness and intimacy of the viewing-situation frequently concealed the very private activities of those within them. Such activities provided a physical metaphor for the equally forbidden, but

72

unseen, imaginative experiences enjoyed by audiences as they identified with events on the screen.

Inevitably, there were frequent and vociferous demands for censorship, from private individuals and from such powerful moralizing pressure groups as the Catholic Legion of Decency. The anxieties that prompted censorship were, of course, always about other people. No one seemed to complain that they felt *themselves* to be witlessly driven to debauchery after seeing a Marlene Dietrich movie, but they were very concerned about such things happening to others. For example, many men worried about how portrayals of independent female sexuality would affect their wives, or about the threat to American manhood presented by a character such as the sexually and ethnically ambiguous figure of Rudolph Valentino. But, apart from the disturbing effect of some movies to traditional gender roles, there was also the problem for parents of whether their children were being initiated through film into what they felt was the potentially corrupting world of adult sexuality. In *Middletown*, a study of American society in the late 1920s, Robert and Helen Lynd reported the anxieties of some high-school teachers who felt that movies were a powerful factor in breaking down social taboos and encouraging what was then considered precocious sexual behaviour in the young.[1]

But, as well as being a source of serious anxieties, the movies were also a provider of great pleasures. They were in consequence a source of often ambivalent feelings, and it was the task of the film industry to resolve the ambivalence. The problem was that anxieties and pleasures frequently had the same source. To eradicate erotic imagery and references to sex would lessen patriarchal and parental fears, but it would also remove a great deal of the enjoyment to be found in the cinematic experience. Often it was depictions of activities and events forbidden in real life that were so exciting to see on screen. Dangerous pleasures could be vicariously enjoyed and the possibilities of an existence outside the boundaries of a traditional family structure imaginatively explored. What was more, this could be done without risk of such experiments being discovered. It was always possible to deny the level of psychological involvement that movies invited, and it was the possibility of denial which provided the film industry with the solution to its problem.

Indeed, it could be said that the industry institutionalized the possibility of denial with the introduction of the Production Code in the 1930s. A fundamental principle of the Code insisted that no picture should be produced which would lower the moral standards of those who saw it. Yet it was clear to everyone that it could only work effectively by acknowledging the economic imperatives of the film industry. To function commercially Hollywood had to provide an enjoyable experience for as large an audience as possible. In effect, Hollywood was doing more than producing films; it was selling the concept of mass entertainment to a vast audience of varying sensibilities, and in sometimes paradoxical ways the activities of the Production Code Administration assisted in this process. In effect, once a film was passed by the Hays Office (named after Will Hays, the industry executive and author of the Code) it received a moral stamp of approval that had a double advantage for the film industry. For while the existence and activities of the Production Code helped to soothe public anxieties, the act of passing a movie meant that the responsibility of determining meaning was subtly shifted from the film-maker to the individual spectator.

This process, which Ruth Vasey has called the "principle of deniability," assisted the creation of ambiguous texts.[2] Forbidden ideas could be disguised and coded into film texts in such a way that they were unlikely to be discovered by any but those who cared to look for them. Richard Maltby has remarked that:

> Once the limits of explicit "sophistication" had been established, the production industry had to find ways of appealing to both "innocent" and "sophisticated" sensibilities in the same object without transgressing the boundaries of public acceptability. This involved devising systems and codes of representation in which "innocence" was inscribed into the text while "sophisticated" viewers were able to "read into" movies whatever meanings they were pleased to find, so long as producers could use the Production Code to deny that they had put them there.

74

Even if unsuitable values or shades of eroticism were to be discovered, it could be argued that it was unintended and that only the most prurient imagination could interpret such scenes as indecent. By means of a series of signs and conventions the movie industry could cater for a range of moral sensibilities, but without being accused of corrupting the innocent or inciting unacceptable behavior in the less "controllable" elements of society. In consequence, the process of adapting to the Production Code was far more subtle and complex than just deleting "offensive" material, and those in the Hays Office cannot be cast in the simple roles of kill-joys out to ruin everyone's fun. The Code was established, as Maltby has shown, as an "instrument of an agreed industry-wide policy, not as the originating source of that policy." Its implementation was part of an elaborate system of negotiation between the film industry and its myriad audience.[3] With this in mind, one can see that it would perhaps be more accurate to view those who implemented the Code not just as censors, but rather as mediators who often helped to steer a way through the problem of deciding what was acceptable to show on screen. Furthermore, their value to the industry was enormous. They helped further develop the double life of overt denial and covert signification which allowed spectators to repudiate and enjoy certain pleasures simultaneously.

The musical was a genre that lent itself well to this double life. Musical numbers allowed a break from the realism of the narrative and provided a means by which censorable thoughts and feelings could find expression through the medium of song and dance. When Fred Astaire begins to sing "Night and Day" to Ginger Rogers in *The Gay Divorcee* (1934), or when the couple whirl into their dance for "Cheek to Cheek" (*Top Hat*), the linear activity of simply following a narrative opens out and changes into an emotional plateau. Whether the number advances the narrative or not, emotional energies are heightened by the music, creating the possibility of a more intense spectator identification with the images on screen. Under these circumstances it is not difficult to interpret many of the Astaire/Rogers dances as displaced sexual activity. Indeed, Dennis Giles has looked at the way that the musical form itself

75

was one in which a concealed discourse on sexuality was likely to occur; and Rick Altman has suggested that the decline of the musical, occurring at the same time as the development of a less repressive morality, was no coincidence but a confirmation of the musical's significance as a means of conceiving aspects of sexuality that could not normally be discussed.[4]

In a way social dancing was itself a code and can be seen as an indicator of sexual ideology and gender relations in a much broader context than the dance-hall. It was an awareness of this that led to public dance-halls, as well as movie-houses, being the targets of serious reformist anxieties. Lewis A. Erenberg writes about the "dance madness" that affected people from every class during the 1920s and brought them flocking to the dance halls, hotel ballrooms, and cabarets. This cultural phenomenon was characterized by social dance forms that had their origins in Black American culture rather than the more formal European styles. This in itself made them suspect for the moral custodians of white society, for, as Erenberg describes, there was a sense of vitality and freedom in these dances that expressed a new age of social relations:

> The acceptance of black music and dance paralleled and drew upon a reevaluation of the previous formalism between men and women. The wonderful nomenclature of the dances, taken from the barnyard, added to the general tone of exuberance, unpretentiousness, and informality between the sexes. Doing the turkey trot, grizzly bear, monkey glide, bunny hug, lame duck, or fox-trot, whites did movements that placed them closer to the natural processes of the animal kingdom than to the restrained pinnacle of the genteel hierarchy that they and well-to-do women had occupied in the Victorian era.... Their liberation found their way into dance and into social relations. The new dances were part of the rebellion against the older sexual mores.[5]

For working-class women the dance-hall culture played an important part in challenging old patterns of behavior and providing a means by which new values could be expressed. As Kathy Peiss has shown, ballrooms and dance palaces provided a new, more publicly social space for women. This not only enhanced their participation in life outside the home but reinforced modern values to do with leisure, sexuality, and personal fulfilment.[6]

Both sexes enjoyed the dance craze but there were broader social implications involved for women. Gaylyn Studlar has remarked that "because dance was so closely associated with a heightened awareness of the body, its fascination for women was noted with varying degrees of alarm," driving one Catholic clergyman to assert that some dances ranked with adultery as a violation of the seventh commandment. The particular appeal of dancing for women, and the suggestion that it plays an important part in the fantasies of many, can be seen to have provided a highly charged cultural context into which Rudolph Valentino, as dancer turned actor, appeared. The tremendous popularity of his style, which included an important element of dance, became in turn a part of the historical, social and artistic background for Astaire's entrance into movies a few years later. Dance was an extra dimension within which performers and spectators could explore ideas that, for one reason or another, were difficult to verbalize. It was the dance element of Valentino's performance, Studlar suggests, that allowed the full potency of his sexual persona to be enjoyed by audiences. This was especially so in scenes such as the "rape" in *Son of the Sheik* (1926) where his portrayal of an extreme masculine sexuality was contained within a stylized balletic sequence:

> Because of the quality of movement displayed, the scene could hardly be read as being a realistic depiction of sexual assault. Through dance-like movement and repose ... the scene may work to make violence acceptable to the film's female audience by controlling and containing the vicious and brutal aspects of male behaviour that women might find objectionable or offensive.[7]

Dance, then, had a variety of cultural functions in both social terms and as a performance art. For the individual it could be a means of casting off old restraints and liberating oneself within a social situation, but its formal properties could also be used to contain imagery and ideas that otherwise might be unacceptable. The ideas and qualities that could be expressed through dance covered a whole range, from the lewd to the purely aesthetic, where its inherent sensuality could be tamed or hidden within its status as art.

The dance team of Irene and Vernon Castle played an important part in making the wilder social dances of their day more acceptable to white society. By refining the display of passion associated with Latin and Black dances they attached more spiritual and ethereal values to the body and the way that it could move. It was a project which, Robert Lawson-Peebles suggests, Fred Astaire took further "by unifying tap with ballroom dancing, thereby transforming tap from a percussive acrobatics to a nimble form of levitation."[8] Originally a Black vernacular dance, the rhythms and energy of tap combined with ballroom dancing to provide the scope for a more dramatic form of dance. It was therefore possible to express a greater range of feelings between couples than straight ballroom dancing could convey, partly because it allowed for individualistic as well as paired dancing. The fact that Astaire and Rogers sometimes dance apart makes the sequences when they are together that much more meaningful. The exact interpretation of that meaning was something that individual viewers could decide for themselves.

Keeping in mind the different types and levels of emotional involvement invited by movies plus the dynamic cultural environment in which they were viewed, one can see that there were ways in which both "sophisticated" and "innocent" pleasures could be derived from watching Astaire and Rogers dance together. In their first movie together, *Flying Down to Rio* (1933), dancing is clearly a potent means of sensual expression. There is a sequence where they watch other couples enjoying the Carioca, a dance which demands that the forehead of each dancer is pressed against that of the partner. After a while Rogers asks what the point of that particular gesture is. "It's to do with mental telepathy" says Astaire; to which Rogers replies, "I can tell what they're thinking about from here." We then see a woman looking at her partner with a shocked expression and slapping his face, to resume the dance in the same way as before. The message is clear. The dancing evokes sexual thoughts and desires that warrant disapproval in terms of contemporary social codes but which are irresistibly enjoyable.

When Astaire and Rogers go onto the floor they emphasize the pleasure of bodies touching in this way by shaking their fingers as though to suggest the "electrifying" sensation it produced. They dance for only a few minutes, but such was the potency of the encounter that the response of the audience engendered the whole series of movies that followed.

The connection between popular music and sex has always been close. In the 1920s the expression to "jazz" with someone was a colloquial term for engaging in sexual activity with them; in the 1950s "Rock'n Roll" had a similar meaning. When Ginger Rogers sings "Music Makes Me Do Things That I Shouldn't Do" in *Flying Down to Rio* we are left in little doubt about what those things might be. In their next film, *The Gay Divorcee* (1934), the lyrics in the Betty Grable/Edward Everett Horton number "Let's Knock Knees" are marginally more subtle than "Music Makes Me Do Things," but there is the added implication of sexual union in the apparently innocent physical contact of "knocking knees." The significance of this number is to establish the hotel in which the movie is set as a place of sexual opportunity, something which was conveyed far more blatantly through dialogue and gesture in the earlier movie. By the time *Top Hat* was released, the following year in 1935, the Production Code was in full force and would therefore have prohibited such references. But by this time they were probably not necessary. All that was needed were reminders to jog the memories of those who had seen the earlier movies. Examples of this would be Rogers' arrival in Astaire's room late at night only to complain about the noise he is making, or when she concocts a story about an affair they did not have in Paris. In this way the audience is offered the spectacle of Rogers' appearance in Astaire's bedroom in her negligée, and the possibility of sexual impropriety in Paris, but without anything actually happening. The spectator is left to consume and manage such images and ideas according to personal predilections.

Aside from his dancing, it would be difficult to find a more unlikely screen lover than Astaire. With his thinning hair, good-natured yet foolish grin and skinny, almost elfin body, he is hard to imagine as anyone's fantasy figure. Yet the films in which he appeared are still regarded as romantic. He has a likable boyish quality even when middle-aged that seems to deny anything more threatening than a playful mischievousness. Nowhere can one find a hint of the sexual menace that was so much a part of Valentino's persona or the all-American machismo appeal of Clark Gable. Even so, there is something that all three share. Each of them portrays in different ways a mastery of the body, their own and often that of a female partner that suggests, with Gable and Valentino particularly, not only the power to be strong but, more potently, the power to be gentle. Tenderness in such men is never seen as a weakness but as an indication of a more complete range of emotional responses. As a focus of audience identification they offer the spectator a means by which a whole spectrum of feelings may be imaginatively explored, bounded only by the limits of desire itself.

This may be harder to see in the persona of Astaire because it exists in reverse form to the way that it appears in Valentino and Gable. With them it is their gentleness that is hidden, the discovery of which imbues their characters with a thrilling potential. With Astaire it is his power as a dynamic and undoubtedly masculine figure that is magically revealed when he begins to dance. Valentino and Gable are conspicuous versions of, respectively, a problematic and a conventional masculinity, and as such are perhaps more obvious subjects for the current discourse on reassessing representations of masculinity.[9] Unlike them, it is not the appearance of Astaire's body that suggests sexuality, but rather the transforming effect of his movements, the way that he behaves in dance. Through his performances we see how the musical offers a different emphasis on masculinity and a potentially more ambivalent form in which it can be displayed. In a sense, the lack of realism in song and dance numbers acts as a means by which underlying sexual motivations can be both masked and revealed, depending on what the viewer wants or expects to find. In terms of the film industry's need to provide both a pleasurable viewing experience for a largely female audience and to meet the requirements of the Production Code, the asexual persona of Astaire was a perfect cover for the erotic significance of much of his dancing.

The possibilities of interpreting him in this way are not only to be found when he dances with a female partner, but are suggested in some of his solos. The "Top Hat" number, in the film of the same name, is a case in point. Steven Cohan suggests that props are often used "to compensate for the female partner's absence." Such props—Cohan instances the hat rack in *Royal Wedding* (1951)—become a fetish, making provocative hints of autoeroticism. Cohan here acknowledges the work of Linda Williams on pornographic film, *Hard Core*. Williams proposes an analogy between the musical and pornography, suggesting, amongst other things, that the solo number of a musical is a "song or dance of self-love and enjoyment."[10] Given the phallic symbolism of Astaire's cane in "Top Hat," the implications would seem to be even more powerful than those suggested by Cohan and Williams. When Astaire uses the cane to "shoot" every other man on the stage and then effortlessly tosses it up into the air and catches it again, he seems to be demonstrating a potency and (sexual) competence that is compelling and impressive. That he finishes by "shooting" male members of the audience seems to confirm his sexual superiority in a way that would not have worked had he "shot" women. But it is when Astaire dances with a partner such as Ginger Rogers that the erotic potential of his dancing is fully apparent, and he becomes a particular kind of spectacle of masculinity.

In her highly influential essay "Visual Pleasure and Narrative Cinema," Laura Mulvey sets out her belief, based in psychoanalytic theory, that all viewing is a masculine activity, and that what is being viewed is inevitably feminine.[11] On the other hand, Steven Cohan suggests that through the musical Astaire becomes the spectacle in a way that tends to subvert these traditional ideas:

> This Hollywood genre actually differs from others because it features men in showstopping numbers as well as women. In making such a blatant spectacle of men, the musical thus challenges the very gendered division of labor which it keeps reproducing in its generic plots... [The song-and-dance-man] therefore finds himself in rather problematic territory—at least as far as film theory is concerned—for the genre has placed him in the very position which the representation system of classic Hollywood cinema has traditionally designated as "feminine."[12]

81

To which I would add that, for the movie to work—not just as a musical performance but as a love story—it requires the audience, both male and female, to watch Astaire through the eyes of a female spectator. Not one who is seeing him perform as a "Song-and-Dance-Man" in the way that Cohan describes, but rather a woman who is forming an emotional attachment to him. In terms of the sexual/visual dynamics between Astaire, Rogers and the audience there is a sense in which Rogers masculinizes Astaire for the spectator with her gaze. This has less to do with him as a spectacle through being a musical performer and more to do with the particular persona of Astaire. If Rogers were to look at a sexually charismatic character such as Gable with the same suppressed desire that she directs at Astaire, it would invite a response that could not be shown. By matching her passion Gable would make Rogers appear vampish, while not responding to her would mean either denying the power of feminine sexuality—which in the context of a love story would work against Hollywood conventions—or would damage Gable's persona as a "real" man. In the case of Astaire, a strong response is not expected, thus allowing Rogers to express her attraction to him, creating, as she does so, Astaire as a believable object of desire for the audience.

Such an interpretation is a greater challenge to the assumptions of Mulvey's article than Cohan's argument, because it not only places Astaire in the position of sexual spectacle but makes Rogers the agent of meaning for the spectator. It often seems to be precisely this construction and portrayal of feminine power that psychoanalytic theory seems so inadequate to describe. Mulvey uses it to present the process of patriarchal control of femininity through the male gaze. But the language and terms of psychoanalysis are so biased towards male domination that it seems an inadequate tool with which to discover any creative feminine activity either on or off the screen. Rather than dismantling patriarchy by looking for ways in which it might be subverted, those who use psychoanalytic theory seem at times to run the risk of simply re-stating the aims of male chauvinism and, despite the critical attack, leaving no active role for women. Undoubtedly, this much-applied theory has a value in providing a model with which to describe and understand the patriarchal obsession with power, but it doesn't adequately deal with the actual experience of those being controlled. The way that such an inferior social position feels and is managed requires its own language and cannot be properly presented in the terminology of the dominant party. Mulvey's description of how patriarchy defines woman is clearly condemning in tone, but to some extent it seems as though one is listening to a description of a prison, when what one really wants to know is how to get out:

> Woman then stands in patriarchal culture as signifier for the male other, bound by a symbolic order in which man can live out his phantasies and obsessions through linguistic command by imposing them on the silent image of woman still tied to her place as bearer of meaning, not maker of meaning.[13]

This presents the single-minded view which comes from the centre of power and which, by definition, cannot look out on life from any other point. Being both central and powerful, such a view assumes an omnipotence and ubiquity which is actually an illusion, and which inhibits exploration of alternative ways of seeing. Yet the complicity required by the patriarchy from those who are subjected to it means that the oppressed must have at least two views and therefore a more diverse and flexible means of identification. They must identify with the centre of power in order to survive, but to deny their own view(s) would be to discount completely the nature of repression. In filmic terms women as an oppressed group are cued to identify with the male gaze, and will see a female character such as Ginger Rogers as an attractive sex-object for men. But they will also be seeking the expression of their own needs and desires by actively identifying with feminine power in whatever form it appears. In the Astaire/Rogers movies it is the medium of dance that allows Astaire to display masculine sexuality, but it is Rogers' response to him that directs the emotional energies of the audience. By means of an analysis of two of their most famous numbers, "Night and Day" and "Cheek to Cheek," we may be able to see how both these factors work in the formulation of Astaire as a focus of erotic pleasure.

"Night and Day" appears in *The Gay Divorcee* as a turning point in the couple's relationship. Up until then, Astaire appears as something of a fool. He tears Rogers' dress, runs into her car and pursues her to no effect at all. Finally catching up with her, he persuades her to dance—and by the end she appears to be in love with him. So what has happened? Or, more to the point, what do we believe, imagine and feel has happened? In "Night and Day," as in "Cheek to Cheek," there is a move from a public to a private space, giving the audience a sense that we are privy to a situation that is becoming ever more intimate. In other words, we discover ourselves as voyeurs. This is emphasized in "Night and Day" when, part way through the dance, the camera moves outside the private space to view the couple through the Venetian blinds of a window. The whole dance is an enactment of a seduction, with Rogers's initial reluctance gradually being broken down so that eventually she allows herself to be held close by Astaire, her body moving in harmony with his. Just before the dance begins, Astaire appears to be unable to assert his desire for Rogers effectively. "Don't ask me to stay," she says. "Alright, I won't," he replies. She turns away, but the rhythm of their movements is choreographed as a prelude to a dance. He becomes more positive, saying: "Don't go; I've so many things to say to you." Then he begins to sing. She listens for a while, but eventually this is not enough and she turns to leave. At this point Astaire physically prevents her from going, in a way that would be impossible for his non-dancing character to do. No matter which direction she turns, he stands between her and her exit. We see this from several angles. At one point we are behind Astaire seeing the large black outline of his outstretched arms across the small, light image of Rogers as she approaches. He then catches hold of her hand and pulls her towards him—and suddenly they are in each others arms, moving together in perfect harmony. Again she tries to leave, even at one point pushing Astaire across the room, but still he persists and gradually wins her over. They dance together as the music builds to a crescendo, and then as it dies Astaire gently lays Rogers back on a seat, dusts his hands as though to suggest that he has achieved what he wanted, and then offers Rogers a cigarette. Her expression through this is of someone dazed with pleasure and transformed in terms of how she feels about her partner. One is left with the feeling that more has happened to her than just a dance.

Despite all the sexual tension that has been transmitted, the body and face of Astaire resists any hint of the iconic identification with sexuality that surrounded Rudolph Valentino. Throughout all his movies, Astaire's body remains asexual and ethereal. Not only do we never see him heaving with passion, as we do Valentino, he does not even become breathless. His movements seem totally without effort, gravity-defying, and magical. By contrast Rogers, for all her competence as a dancer, seems earth-bound and ordinary, like us. When Astaire sweeps her off her feet and metaphorically seduces her, he retains an innocence that would not have been possible with other male stars. If one saw Valentino performing a similar dance with the climactic music, deep back bends and emotionally-dazed partner at the end, it is difficult to imagine anything other than a sexual interpretation being possible. Indeed, the Valentino "rape" scene and the "Night and Day" number provide similar opportunities for erotic fantasy, but they achieve it in significantly different ways. Whereas, in *Son of the Sheik*, the implicit sexual violence of the scene and persona of Valentino may be contained within the concept of dance, the erotic nature of the Astaire/Rogers dance is contained by Astaire's ethereal, asexual style. With Valentino the sexually-charged atmosphere created in his movies had a direct focus on his persona in a very physical sense, but with Astaire sexuality is always diffuse and abstract, finding its main focus in the way that Rogers responds to him.

We see this particularly in "Cheek to Cheek." In this dance there is a pattern similar to that described in "Night and Day": a move into a private space initially denied to the audience, but which it later invades. In a way this dance seems to cover what has happened between the characters earlier in the movie and there is a sequence that is reminiscent of the earlier dance, "Isn't it a Lovely Day," where they dance together but with very little physical contact. "Cheek to Cheek" moves through that stage and we see the relationship between the dancers becoming increasingly intimate and passionate as the music builds to a climax. At the point of climax Astaire lifts Rogers up into the air and the dance finishes with a deep back-bend where Rogers is in a position of complete passive surrender to the dominant masculine stance he adopts. Everything stops and we, like the dancers/lovers, are held in the moment. In the last few bars of the music the couple gently dance over to the edge of the floor and again there is silence—no music, no dialogue, just the emotionally charged atmosphere created by the dance. The camera is focussed on Rogers's face, and her expression seems to confirm that this was not merely a dance but a deeply significant and transforming event in her life. She looks at Astaire as though seeing him for the first time. She recognises him as something other than she thought, and the camera—lingering on her face—cues the audience to also look at him as she does, as more than a dancer.

It is these moments that are so complex, both emotionally and in terms of film theory. Superficially, they conform to the traditional idea of the female as spectacle, with Astaire (and the audience) occupying the role of masculine spectator. But even though the camera is dwelling on Rogers's face, what we are looking at is her watching Astaire. Her expression defies us to see her as merely the object of our gaze, but rather suggests that Astaire has become an object of visual and emotional fascination for her and, through audience identification, for the viewer as well. Before the narrative picks up again at the end of "Cheek to Cheek" there is a full twelve seconds in which nothing happens except this act of looking. The silence is intense, almost embarrassing, as though for those seconds we, and the movie, are in danger of somehow being exposed. We can only see Astaire with his back half-turned to us, but for those moments he retains the masculine power he has acquired through the dance. As soon as we see him full-face again he is transformed back into the boyish, friendly, slightly foolish character that he was before. In other words, once Astaire has stopped dancing we can only enjoy the spectacle of his masculine sexuality by seeing it reflected through Rogers's expression as she looks at him.

It would seem, then, that even within the Hollywood romance tradition of "boy sees girl, chases girl, and finally gets girl,"

Rogers can be seen both as a creator of meaning and as an indicator of active female spectatorship. In a sense the movie uses the implicit assumptions of patriarchy, of the woman as a passive object of the male gaze, to conceal the power that she has to eroticize Astaire and to trigger the possibility of a more "sophisticated" interpretation of the movie. If Mulvey's assertion, that it is not expected for a woman to be a "maker of meaning," is true, then its occurrence is likely to be registered at a less conscious level and therefore to pass relatively unnoticed. To some extent, patriarchy is similar to censorship in seeking to control what we see and how we see it. But, as I have tried to demonstrate, Hollywood cinema makes use of repression, or rather the emotional energy that it generates, to invite a greater imaginative involvement on the part of the spectator. By providing imagery, sequences, and plots that are ambiguous and overdetermined it creates a dynamic environment in which a number of interpretations are possible. To be sure, dance was given a respectable front by the sexually innocuous figure of Astaire; but by following Rogers's cue it is possible to see through the disguise. The small effort involved would perhaps discourage those who enjoyed an "innocent" view of the movie from seeking a more "sophisticated" subtext, but for others the search and illicit disclosure of erotic imagery would only increase its potency.

In this way the movie industry sought to please us all. While serving only one real master, that of capital, it pretended to love everyone by whispering to each that our most forbidden desires could be enjoyed and yet our most private thoughts remain undisclosed. Conspirator and confidante, Hollywood cinema invited a partnership between itself and its audience that simply became more subtle under censorship, drawing upon an even greater degree of imaginative and emotional involvement from the individual spectator. For women who were experiencing the additional restrictions created by men there was an even greater need to seek some kind of outlet for their frustrations. From this point of view it could be argued that those who felt comfortable with the dominant ideology were the more passive consumers of the values on offer. In contrast, the imagination of women and other repressed groups was inevitably more active in subverting texts, looking for alternatives and seeking the pleasurable release that their situation demanded and that movies promised to provide. In trying to be all things to all men, and perhaps even more so to all women, Hollywood was extraordinarily successful in making good that promise to millions, who in various ways, whether they knew it or not, always went to see "movies in disguise."

NOTES

1 Robert and Helen Lynd, *Middletown: A Study in Contemporary American Culture* (New York: Harcourt, Brace and World, 1929), p. 267.

2 Ruth Vasey, *Diplomatic Representations: Mediations Between Hollywood and its Global Audiences 1922–1939* (Unpublished PhD Thesis, Exeter University, 1990), p. 140.

3 Richard Maltby, "The Production Code and the Hays Office," Tino Balio et al., *Grand Design: Hollywood as a Modern Business Enterprise* (New York: Scribner's, 1993), pp. 40–41, 38.

4 Rick Altman, introductory comment, and Dennis Giles, "Show-Making," *Genre: The Musical*, ed. Rick Altman (London: Routledge and Kegan Paul, 1981), pp. 85–101.

5 Lewis A. Erenberg, *Steppin' Out: New York Nightlife and the Transformation of American Culture, 1890–1930* (Chicago: University of Chicago Press, 1981), p. 154.

6 Kathy Peiss, *Cheap Amusements* (Philadelphia: Temple University Press, 1986), p. 90.

7 Gaylyn Studlar, "Valentino, 'Optic Intoxication' and Dance Madness," *Screening the Male*, ed. Steven Cohan and Ina Rae Hark (London: Routledge, 1993), pp. 24, 35. On the appeal of dance to women, see Angela McRobbie, "*Fame, Flashdance*, and Fantasies of Achievement," *Fabrications: Costume and the Female Body*, ed. J. Gaines and C. Herzog (New York: Routledge, 1990), particularly pp. 41–4.

8 Robert Lawson-Peebles, "Performance Arts," *Modern American Culture: An Introduction*, ed. Mick Gidley (London: Longman, 1993), p. 275.

9 On Valentino, see Gaylyn Studlar, "The Perils of Pleasure? Fan Magazine Discourse as Women's Commodified Culture in the 1920s," *Wide Angle* Vol. 13, No. 1 (January 1991); Studlar, "Valentino, 'Optic Intoxication' and Dance Madness;" and Miriam Hansen, *Babel and Babylon* (Cambridge, MA: Harvard University Press, 1991). On Clark Gable, see Joe Fisher, "Clark Gable's Balls: Real Men Never Lose Their Teeth," *You Tarzan: Masculinity, Movies and Men*, ed. Pat Kirkham and Janet Thumim (London: Lawrence & Wishart, 1993), pp. 35–51.

10 Steven Cohan, "'Feminising' the Song-and-Dance-Man," *Screening the Male*, ed. Cohan and Hark, p. 55. Linda Williams, *Hard Core: Power, Pleasure, and the "Frenzy of the Visible"* (London: Pandora Press, 1990), p. 133.

11 Laura Mulvey, "Visual Pleasure and Narrative Cinema," *Film Theory and Criticism*, ed. Gerald Mast and Marshal Cohen (3rd edn., New York: Oxford University Press, 1985), pp. 803–16.

12 Cohan, "'Feminising' the Song-and-Dance-Man," pp. 46–7.

13 Mulvey, "Visual Pleasure and Narrative Cinema," p. 804.

7

Brush Up Your Shakespeare:
The Case of *Kiss Me, Kate*

Robert Lawson-Peebles

Shakespeare and the Street

Brush up your Shakespeare,
Start quoting him now.
Brush up your Shakespeare
And the women you will wow.
With the wife of the British embessida
Try a crack out of "Troilus and Cressida,"
If she says she won't buy it or tike it
Make her tike it, what's more, "As You Like It."
If she says your behavior is heinous
Kick her right in the "Coriolanus."
Brush up your Shakespeare
And they'll all kowtow.[1]

Cole Porter's lyric invokes two cultural milieux and two appropriate modes of action. They are deliberately constructed so as
to be in conflict. The more obvious cultural milieu is American.
It is strongly masculinist and domineering. In this refrain it is
violently aggressive, while in others it is overtly phallic. It is
conveyed in the vernacular of the street, emphasized by rhymes
which draw on dialect (wow/kowtow) or which work only
through perversion of received pronunciation (tike it/like it).

89

The other cultural milieu is English in origin and feminine. It too has its own language, once again emphasized by rhymes. "Heinous" is a loan-word, from the fourteenth-century French "haineus" (hateful). Here the speaker has borrowed it again, from the literary culture of the wife of the British Ambassador, but he repays her with more than interest. "Embessida," like "tike," rhymes only as a perversion, but this time the perversion is a parody of the language of the English aristocracy, represented abroad by officials of the British Diplomatic Service.

The allusion to the Ambassador is particularly important because it conjures up an image of the leading edge of British imperial power. Today, although that power has disappeared, the Diplomatic Service is still in vestigial place. In 1948, when Porter wrote the lyric, it was waning but still important. In the lyric, however, it is inferior to the power invoked by the name of Shakespeare. The importance of this power is signalled by the regular repetition of the name throughout the lyric, and by what it will achieve: the pleasures of sexual domination, the joys of inflicting pain on a social superior. But it is the three words preceding the proper noun which are most important of all. "Brush up" indicates two things. It refers to the text in which the works of Shakespeare are printed, and which must be renewed by receiving fresh attention; and it refers to the revitalized knowledge, and hence power, of the reader. The text, and the power derived from it, is universally available—hence the possessive adjective "your." Shakespeare can be used, not just by the wives of British Ambassadors, nor just by the British, but by everyone. His works exist in both a universal and a superior realm. In consequence they unite the two milieux. They allow the American street to make contact with and dominate the British Embassy.

In this essay I would like to suggest some of the ways in which Shakespeare's potency is realized. I will try to do this by means of a detailed analysis of the film version of *Kiss Me, Kate* (1953), the Cole Porter musical in which "Brush Up Your Shakespeare" appears. It was issued by MGM, produced by Jack Cummings, and directed by George Sidney. Before I look at the film, however, I would like to set it, and my opening points, in critical context. Porter's interpretation of the power of

Shakespeare seems, at first sight, to be so extreme that it could only be a joke. Indeed, for a number of critics it is a bad joke. In their view the gap between the cultures symbolized by the Embassy and the street is so great that it cannot be bridged. The two cultures are tagged with the polarizing adjectives "high" and "low" and are regarded as eternally at war. The literary critic I. A. Richards, for instance, drew a clear distinction between "popular taste" and "trained discrimination," and believed that the latter was being subverted by "the more sinister potentialities of the cinema." T. S. Eliot, who was more receptive to some elements of "low" culture, nevertheless rejected its more modern manifestations. In an essay on the music-hall comedienne Marie Lloyd, Eliot regarded with horror "the encroachment of the cheap and rapid-breeding cinema." Richards and Eliot wrote these remarks in the mid-1920s, and their imagery of a malign and quickly proliferating organism was no doubt due to the fast growth of cinema-going. Yet over forty years later F. R. Leavis adopted a similar position when he attacked Ken Russell's proposed film of Lawrence's *Women in Love* as "an obscene undertaking."[2]

Even those critics interested in film have tended to operate from a polarized model. Leo Braudy, for instance, distinguishes between "classic films" which trace their lineage back to the European Romantic cult of the personal creative sensibility and "genre films" such as westerns and musicals which tend towards the formulaic. Stanley Kauffmann has asserted that "the film medium and Shakespeare are born antagonists; no Shakespearean film has ever proved otherwise." The pioneering French director Ferdinand Zecca went further; he regarded Shakespeare as an incompetent, a "wretched fellow" who "left out the most marvellous things" from his plays. The movie moguls tended to agree. They thought of the Bard as bad box office, and no more than an excuse, as the chairman of Columbia put it, to have "a bunch of guys running around in their knickers."[3]

The polarity between "high" and "low" is, however, no more than a model, and it is possible to formulate an alternative. The alternative, interestingly, is to be found in the work of T. S. Eliot. As we have seen, Eliot was attracted to old-fashioned forms of "low" culture. Perhaps this prompted him to devise a means of bridging the gap. The means is to be found in his 1940 essay "What Is A Classic?" Writing with a wartime awareness of the values of a culture which was under attack, Eliot suggested that Virgil was the classic writer which no modern culture could hope to match. Nevertheless, he added, "each literature has its greatness, not in isolation, but because of its place in a larger pattern." Modern writers therefore partook of a power whose source could be traced back to Virgil. In so partaking they reformulated aspects of Virgil's greatness in a different language, a modern style, a contemporary vernacular. In short, they brought Virgil up to date.[4]

The English critic Frank Kermode has developed Eliot's ideas further, briefly in the Preface to his edition of Eliot's essays and at greater length in *The Classic* (1975) and *Forms of Attention* (1985). Kermode suggests that there are two ways of looking at a classic. The first regards it "as a closed book that learning can partly open." The second sees it as "a more or less open text from which new readings may generate." The first view regards the classic as a sacred text to which only a privileged few are given the key. The second view looks on it as a text which is eternally relevant and which by a process of accommodation to the present is available to a much larger circle. The "permanent value" of *Hamlet*, therefore, is its "perpetual modernity." A classic achieves that status because it is protean. It obligingly changes its shape so that it offers up new meanings to a new group of interpreters.[4]

Kermode's remarks can, in turn, be developed further. Shakespeare is a figure of such protean power that he lends himself to both models that I have sketched out. According to the first, Shakespeare's genius resides in his words. The acolyte is therefore a reader who enters into solitary communion with the Bard. This model draws much of its strength from the Romantic cult of the creative imagination. As Peter Conrad has shown, the cult developed further in operatic versions of Shakespeare, which treated the plays as lyrical monologues or as frustrated novels. Above all, this view of Shakespeare denies the dramatic elements in the plays. It lends itself, on the one hand, to the belief in the central moral value of practical criticism as a means of understanding the text. It is worth remembering that much of the work that is still done in university English departments has developed from the pioneering practical criticism of Richards and Leavis. On the other hand, this view allows critics like Leo Braudy to distinguish between "classic" films and "genre" films, and directors like Ferdinand Zecca to write Shakespeare off as a poor playwright.[6]

The other model of Shakespeare asserts that, more than anything else, he is a dramatist. The words on the page are, finally, inadequate. They are little more than stage directions, shadows of dramatic potency. This view of Shakespeare draws much of its power from remarks by the Austrian philosopher Ludwig Wittgenstein:

> Shakespeare displays the dance of human passions, one might say. Hence he has to be objective; otherwise he would not so much display the dance of human passions—as talk about it. But he displays it to us in a dance, not naturalistically.

The essence of Shakespeare is therefore beyond words, the medium of talk. It exists, rather, in spatial representations. Here Wittgenstein uses the image of the dance. Elsewhere he refers to the Bard as a painter and a dreamer. It is appropriate, therefore, that his remarks do not take the literary form of ordered explication, but rather appear as scattered aphorisms in his manuscripts. It is appropriate, too, that amongst the manuscripts is a refusal to believe in the "enormous amount of praise" that has been "lavished on Shakespeare without understanding and for the wrong reasons by a thousand professors of literature." Fortunately, some literary critics have in recent years been listening to Wittgenstein.[7]

This second view of Shakespeare, by treating him as a dramatist, makes him available to a large audience and therefore both modernizes and democratizes him. It allowed a critic like Jan Kott to call him "our contemporary," and discuss *Hamlet* in the light of the politics of the former Communist bloc. It also opens the way to film and musical versions of the plays. Shakespearean films date back almost to the birth of the industry. Part of the Beerbohm Tree production of *King John* was filmed in 1899, just four years after the start of cinematography. By 1972 some 210 films had treated Shakespearean themes. There are fewer musical versions of the Bard. Rodgers and Hart adapted *The Comedy of Errors* into *The Boys from Syracuse*, which appeared on Broadway in 1938 and was filmed in 1940. The stage production received rave reviews and ran for 235 performances, while the film was nominated for two Oscars. The best known musical, however, is *West Side Story*. The original Broadway production opened in 1957 and ran for 732 performances. The 1961 film was awarded ten Oscars and is ranked as number four in the list of "All-Time Hit Musical Films."[8]

Unfortunately, many Shakespearean productions approach the Bard with (to adopt Wittgenstein's metaphor for a moment) flat feet. They move towards the polarized model I have sketched earlier, and treat Shakespeare with reverence, hoping thereby to assume his mantle of respectability. A well-known example is the 1935 production of *A Midsummer Night's Dream*. Warner Brothers intended it as a "prestige production" in response to the literary pretensions of MGM's Irving Thalberg. The Viennese émigré composer Erich Korngold was hired to rescore Mendelssohn's music. The choreographer was Bronislava Nijinska, wife of Vaslav Nijinsky, who was best known as a dancer and choreographer with Diaghilev's Ballets Russes. The Austrian impresario Max Reinhardt co-directed the film, which starred some of Warner Brothers's most popular and promising actors, including Dick Powell, James Cagney, Joe E. Brown, Mickey Rooney, and Olivia de Havilland, whose first film this was. Warner Brothers even produced a seven-minute newsreel extolling the production values and star-studded première of the film. Yet, apart from some imaginative woodland scenes and the determined hamming of Cagney, the film remained resolutely earthbound. As the critic Gilbert Seldes remarked in 1937, Reinhardt "nearly smothered Shakespeare in textiles."[9] In stark contrast, *Kiss Me, Kate* refuses to treat Shakespeare with reverence. It gambles—and gambols—with its source text, and in consequence is a much greater success. I shall now try to show why.

Hamlet and the Glove-Strip

Kiss Me, Kate is not the first film version of *The Taming of the Shrew*. The play's slapstick, which has sometimes given it a lowly position in the Shakespeare pantheon, has appealed to a number of bolder directors. D. W. Griffith directed a version in 1908. Griffith's protégé, Mary Pickford, starred with her current husband Douglas Fairbanks Sr. in another version in 1929. It was the first talking picture of any Shakespeare play. It is now well-known only because, it is thought, it had the credit-line, "by William Shakespeare, with Additional Dialogue by Sam Taylor." The credit-line is a myth. If the film has to be the butt of snobbery, it should be for a howler committed by Fairbanks when he refuses to allow Pickford to eat meat in Act IV, Scene 1:

> I tell thee, Kate, 'twas burnt and dried away,
> And I expressly am forbid to touch it,
> For it engenders chole*r* and feedeth anger.

Presumably it was choler, rather than any disease, which led to the breakup of the stars' marriage.[10]

What gives *Kiss Me, Kate* its particular flavor is not burnt meat but rather its indebtedness to the long and honourably disreputable tradition of parody. Parody operates by means of incongruity. It presupposes that its audience knows, if only in a general way, the subject which it sets out to mock. The rise of Shakespeare's fame, in part fostered by the Romantics, was therefore matched by the growth of parodic plays, which reached a height in the nineteenth century on both sides of the Atlantic. American parodies were often spiced by anti-British, anti-monarchical sentiments. They, in turn, were parodied by Mark Twain in *Huckleberry Finn*, when the two confidence men, the "Duke" and the "Dauphin," attempt a "Shaksperean Revival!!!" in Arkansas. The tradition continued on film. *Kiss Me, Kate* was immediately preceded by *Casanova in Burlesque*, which lacquered *The Taming of the Shrew* with the hip patina and patois of 1944. It starred Joe E. Brown (perhaps making a bid for a Shakespearean career) and June Havoc, and had songs composed by Jule Styne (better known for *Gentlemen Prefer*

Blondes (1953) and *Funny Girl* (1968)), including one entitled "Willie the Shake."[11]

Parody depends upon the discord that it generates between itself and the original off which it feeds. In *Kiss Me, Kate* the discord is established in the second song, "Too Darn Hot." The setting for the first two songs is the apartment of the actor Fred Graham. The opening shots establish that Fred is successful and sophisticated. The apartment has a balcony which over-looks the other skyscraper apartment blocks of midtown Manhattan. It is expensively furnished, replete with large mirrors, pot plants, photographs of Fred in various roles, a highly polished grand piano, and Paul, an English butler, also highly polished. Opposite the fireplace is a large white settee, and over the fireplace is a large oil painting. Apart from Paul, the place is occupied by Fred, Lilli Vanessi, and "Cole Porter" (played by Ron Randell). They are running through the songs written by Porter for a new show which will star Fred and Lilli: a musical version of *The Taming of the Shrew*. The photographs show that Fred has played a wide variety of parts. In them he is dressed as a cowboy, an officer in the USAAF, and a Southern beau. The oil painting shows that he has realized the dream of every actor, for he has played Hamlet.

The photographs are sketchily suggestive of contemporary movies. The cowboy photograph is, as I will suggest later, almost certainly taken from *Annie Get Your Gun*, released by MGM in 1950. The Southern beau is in the mould of Clark Gable in *Gone With the Wind* (1939); it could possibly be of Gaylord Ravenal in the 1951 MGM production of *Show Boat*. The USAAF officer looks suspiciously like Glenn Miller without glasses. The *Glenn Miller Story* would be released by United Artists in 1954. In contrast, there is nothing sketchy about the painting of Hamlet. It can be identified with absolute precision. It is a likeness of Laurence Olivier in the movie he directed himself in 1948. After the movie's opening scene on the battle-ments, Olivier's camera wanders the labyrinthine castle at Elsinore. It lingers briefly before an ornamented chair in a council chamber. This is the chair on which Hamlet sits during the ensuing scene, and the chair to which he returns at the close of his first soliloquy ("O that this too too sullied flesh..."),

96

his head once again languidly supported by his right hand.[12] The oil painting in Fred Graham's apartment reproduces the chair and the detail of Olivier's costume, including his blond hairstyle. It suggests, though, that Fred played the part, for during the opening sequence Fred pauses briefly before the painting and adopts Hamlet's pose, and "Cole Porter" makes an appropriate obeisance.

The allusion to Olivier is particularly appropriate, because the actor had achieved his preeminence through successful careers both in Hollywood and on the English stage. Those two careers, and the values associated with them, were united in Olivier's highly popular and influential 1944 production of *Henry V*. For the next few years Olivier's appearances on film confirmed that he appealed to discriminating (as Richards would have put it) as well as to popular tastes. In addition to starring in *Hamlet*, he took the leading roles in William Wyler's version of Theodore Dreiser's *Carrie* and in *The Beggar's Opera* (both 1952). This last film united the dual values of Olivier's recent film work. John Gay's original 1728 work was controversial when it first appeared because it dealt with a "low" subject, highwaymen, and mustered the popular songs of the day under the guise of Italian opera.[13] After 1920 it had frequent revivals, with musical scores by Edward Dent, Darius Milhaud, Benjamin Britten and, of course, Kurt Weill. The 1952 film was staged as a vividly technicolored costume drama, with music arranged by Arthur Bliss.

It was understandable, therefore, that Jack Cummings, the producer of *Kiss Me, Kate*, would want to cast Olivier as Fred Graham. Had he succeeded, the oil painting would have become the lynchpin of a system of cross-references as labyrinthine as the castle at Elsinore. Olivier would have played Fred playing Olivier playing Hamlet. As it is, the setting still orchestrates recent cinema history to suggest that Fred amalgamates the qualities of some of the most famous actors of his time. It is a reflection on the recent work of the film's director, George Sidney, who also directed *Annie Get Your Gun* (1946) and *Show Boat*. It is a tribute to him, too. Alain Masson has called Sidney "an activist of *mise-en-scène*."[14] Here he has acted with very great care.

Naturally, it is all a joke; but it is a joke done with subtlety, thereby making it a stark contrast with "Too Darn Hot." The sequence begins when Lois Lane enters the apartment, followed hotfoot by a six-piece combo. She explains that she is between shows at the Copa. She sheds her coat to reveal a crimson tasselled leotard with matching shoes and long gloves. Pausing only to check the contents of Fred's drinks cabinet, she demonstrates her "number." Part of the first verse is typical of the lyric's sexual directness:

> I'd like to stop for my baby tonight,
> And blow my top with my baby tonight,
> But I'd be a flop with my baby tonight,
> 'Cause it's too darn hot.[15]

But it isn't too hot for Lois, whose method combines two ingredients. One is a dazzling display of high-speed tap-dancing. Lois leaps tables and spirals around the settee, much to the astonishment of Fred, Lilli, and "Cole," who are seated on it. The second ingredient is more raunchy. It includes a number of cheesecake positions before the large mirrors; some bumping and grinding; some flirting with Fred and with the camera, assisted by a black lace fan; and a striptease. One by one she removes her gloves, a crimson silk scarf and some jewelry, and hurls it at the camera. Paul, the butler, is rooted to the floor, his face fixed in an expression of Old World horror—for all this, of course, takes place in front of the brooding Danish presence.

The contrast between "high" and "low" is underlined when, for a period of twelve seconds, the camera dollies backwards, pursued by Lois, ogling archly behind her fan. The background is filled with the receding portrait of Hamlet. The band, at this point off-camera, repeat the word "hot" to the insistent beat of bongo-drums. This is followed by an appreciative drawn-out sigh of "cool," which breaks the spell and ushers in a frantic coda. Lois and the band use contemporary musicians' jargon, with phrases like "go girl go" and "crazy, man." At times they are assisted by an offstage swing band with a prominent trumpet section.

"Too Darn Hot" is deliberately garish, but it rests on a web of allusions no less complex than that supporting the portraiture of Fred Graham. The bongos are, I think, a reminder of the beat of the tom-toms which accompany Mary Martin in " Night and Day," the title song of the 1946 biopic of Cole Porter. The trumpets may recall the trumpet-soaked soundtrack in the speakeasy segment of the "Broadway Melody" ballet in *Singin' In the Rain*, released in 1952. But there are clearer allusions. Lois's legs and dress resemble those of Cyd Charisse during that same speakeasy segment. In particular, Lois's glove-strip harks back to a similar performance by Rita Hayworth to the song "Put the Blame on Mame, Boys," in the film *Gilda*. *Gilda* was released in the same year as *Night and Day*, by which time Hayworth had established herself as the supreme siren of 1940s' cinema. She made the front page of *Time* and was the favorite cover-girl for *Life*. Over five million copies of one of her *Life* photographs (in which she wore a black and white negligée) were distributed to servicemen. It received the ultimate military accolade of being pasted to the bomb dropped on Hiroshima, an event that, according to President Truman, was "the greatest thing in history." Indeed, the US Army further heightened the historical imperatives surrounding Rita Hayworth by stencilling the name "Gilda" on the bomb dropped in 1946 on Bikini Atoll. Hayworth heightened them too. She married first Orson Welles and then the Prince Aly Khan, the spiritual leader of the Ismaeli Muslims. She played variations on *Gilda* in several films, and recreated the glove-strip in the 1957 musical *Pal Joey*. That film, appropriately, was directed by George Sidney.[16]

All the World's a Stage—Unquote

The contrasts created in "Too Darn Hot" are developed in the remainder of the film. These are achieved in two ways. The first is through the structure of theme and setting. *Kiss Me, Kate* is within the genre of the backstage musical. The central theme of the film, therefore, concerns the vicissitudes and triumphs involved in staging a musical version of *The Taming of the Shrew*. The virtue of this thematic structure is that it allows the director to exploit the antithesis between the staged production and the apparently "real" life which surrounds it.[17] The setting of "Too Darn Hot," in all its detail, attempts to persuade the viewer that it is "real." So too does the succeeding brief rehearsal sequence at the theater. Thereafter the setting tends towards artificiality. This is particularly the case with the onstage sequences, which use bold sets and brilliant costumes. The opening scene of the production, "We Open in Venice," proclaims that its ultimate subject is acting. The four characters in the scene—Fred, Lilli, Lois and her boyfriend Bill—dance by leaping on and off a moving belt. They are dressed in vermilion jerkins and tights, shoes with exaggerated curled toes, and black hoods which stretch down to their waists. The backdrop moves at the same pace as the belt and is decorated with outline representations of the Italian cities at which the show has appeared. The scene ends when Fred throws a red smoke-bomb at the camera.

The artificiality of the opening scene is maintained throughout the production. The setting of the Paduan street-scenes comprises the pink front of the Minola house; a pink ground on which are painted receding white orthogonals; a flat at midstage containing a triumphal arch; and a backdrop on which are painted two pillars. The set here is similar to those of Olivier's *Henry V* in deliberately recreating a specific pictorial mode. While Olivier looked back to the brothers Limbourg, Froissart, Uccello, and Bruegel, Sidney ultimately recalls the perspective experiments of Quattrocento Florence which had such a marked influence on the Elizabethan stage. Their purposes, however, are quite different. Olivier's sets enrich his film, adding further dimensions to the realism of the initial Globe setting. Sidney alludes to the achievements of the Quattrocento only to mock them. To an extent, his set resembles the Mannerist revolt against the classical style. His stretched pillars resemble those to be found in Pontormo's *Joseph in Egypt* (1517–1518) and Parmigianino's *Madonna of the Long Neck* (c.1535). But he goes even further. From the statue on top of each pillar flies an impossibly long banner. The orthogonals have been stripped of their cross-members and are kinked rightwards in the distance. Finally, the triumphal arch is broken. The mathematical perfection of Piero della Francesca has here been tested to destruction.[18]

An abbreviated version of *The Taming of the Shrew* is played in this garish setting. Some of Shakespeare's lines are used to summarize the plot and push it forward. One or two of them are used in the songs, alongside a pastiche Elizabethan language which is then punctured by a modern cliché. Hence "I've Come to Wive it Wealthily in Padua":

> With a hunny, nunny, nunny,
> And a hey, hey, hey,
> Not to mention money, money
> For a rainy day,
> I've come to wive it wealthily in Padua.

Such deflations are an integral part of the reflexivity which, as Jane Feuer has shown, is an important element of the Hollywood musical. We see the audience on several occasions, and at one point a runway suddenly appears in the midst of the theater. On it, surrounded by the audience, Fred sings "Where Is the Life that Late I Led?" The opening and closing lines only are drawn from *The Taming of the Shrew*. Otherwise, the song runs together references to Broadway (the Shubert Brothers' productions) and recent films (*Gone With the Wind*, *Citizen Kane* (1941)) with glances at street life in Italy and elsewhere:

> Where is Rebecca, my Becki-Weckio,
> Again is she cruising that amusing Ponte Vecchio?
> Where is Fedora, the wild virago?
> It's lucky I missed her gangster sister from Chicago.

Fred sings while straddling a broken arch. At the end of the song a close-up superimposed over a tracking shot transports him weightlessly back to the stage.[19]

Intersecting the production of *The Taming of the Shrew* is a complex backstage plot. Fred and Lilli were once partners both on and off the stage. They are now divorced. Lilli is engaged to a rich Texas cattleman. Fred is flirting with Lois, but Lois is only encouraging him to ensure that she and Bill are included in the

101

show. These convoluted backstage relationships serve in part to highlight the relative simplicity of Shakespeare's plot. After all, Bianca's suitors have simply to carry Katherina off in order to clear the way for their approach to the younger sister. In contrast, modern Manhattan relationships are so embroiled that they threaten to swamp the production. They do so in two ways. First, the ill-feeling between Fred and Lilli erupts on stage at the close of the first Act. He spanks her in front of the audience—much to its amusement—and she quits the show, setting off for Texas with her fiancé in his Jaguar, which is decorated with enormous cowhorns. Second Bill, an inveterate gambler, has signed an IOU in Fred's name. Two hoodlums arrive at the theatre to collect from Fred, but are drawn into taking parts in the production.

The second method used to develop the discords created in "Too Darn Hot" is miscasting, or what Cathy Klaprat has called "offcasting." Offcasting was employed by studios to diversify, as Klaprat put it, "the traits of its product while at the same time invoking the familiar expectations associated with star differentiation."[20] Offcasting lends itself to irony, and perhaps its most ironic usage occurred when Henry Fonda, Hollywood's good guy, played a sadist in Sergio Leone's "Spaghetti Western," *Once Upon a Time in the West* (1968). But in *Kiss Me, Kate* there are offcasting ironies enough. Lois is played by Ann Miller. Miller is a particularly idiosyncratic figure in the history of the musical. Her dancing is so virtuosic that she has been regarded as the sole successor to Eleanor Powell. But she adds to her work a high-voltage sexual charge much more reminiscent of Hayworth than Powell. In consequence she created a niche for herself in the musicals of the 1940s and 1950s. She was contrasted with Judy Garland's introspective figure in *Easter Parade* (1948); and in *On the Town* (1949) she saturated "Prehistoric Man" with sexual energy. In *Kiss Me, Kate* Miller's high profile, displayed to such strong effect in "Too Darn Hot," is repeated in two numbers. The first is "Tom, Dick and Harry" in the staged production, where she makes it clear that she will accept any Paduan man that she can trap with her butterfly net. The second is "Always True to You in My Fashion," where—to Bill's dismay—she flirts briefly with a sailor cast in the likeness of Fred Astaire while she indicates, in some of Porter's most witty lines, that her sights are set much higher:

> Mister Harris, plutocrat,
> Wants to give my cheek a pat,
> If the Harris pat,
> Means a Paris hat,
> Bébé, Oo-la-la!

The irony is that she is cast as Bianca, the younger daughter whom Lucentio calls "this young modest girl" and of whom Hortensio remarks: "Sweet Bianca! Happy man be his dole. He that runs fastest gets the ring." In Sidney's version of Shakespeare's play it is Bianca who does the running.[21]

The inversion is apparent, too, in the casting of Katherina. She is described by Hortensio as:

> intolerable curst,
> And shrewd and froward so beyond all measure
> That, were my state far worser than it is,
> I would not wed her for a mine of gold.

She is played by Kathryn Grayson, who made her career in the 1940s as a sweet young soprano. She is to be seen in this role in *Ziegfeld Follies* (1944), directed by Vincente Minnelli, and in *Thousands Cheer* (1943) and *Anchors Aweigh* (1945), both directed by George Sidney. By 1953 Grayson was 31. She had moved beyond the youthful roles, but Sidney completely fractured her star image by casting her as a spitfire both inside and outside the production of *The Taming of the Shrew*. Grayson plays her part with gusto, particularly when she wrecks the pewter in her solo number, "I Hate Men." But when she is seen in the company of Miller and the male actors who are altogether more substantial and several inches taller, the effect is deliberately ludicrous.[22]

Unfortunately, the care taken in offcasting the female leads is not apparent with the males, and, to this extent, the movie does not parody Shakespeare but simply updates him, transforming the problem facing men in Elizabethan England into the problem facing men in postwar America. Tommy Rall plays the handsome ne'er-do-well Bill with aplomb but without a hint of cynicism. More is made of the character of Fred, although not by offcasting. Howard Keel plays the part with characteristic chest-swelling masculinity, and in this respect he is a postwar Douglas Fairbanks Sr. It is a pity that Keel persuaded Jack Cummings to cast him rather than Olivier. We shall never know what piquant perversities the world's leading Shakespearean actor would have brought to the part. There is just one moment when the casting of Keel makes the proper (or rather, improper) point. It is in the opening sequence, when the setting suggests that Fred is the most wide-ranging actor of his day. There is, too, a hint of those labyrinthine depths I suggested earlier. If the photographs are indeed of *Annie Get Your Gun* and *Show Boat*, then the roles portrayed are those of Frank Butler and Gaylord Ravenal, both played by Keel. In both instances the director, once again, was Sidney. Otherwise, parodic distance is achieved by making Keel look ridiculous. I have already described his first appearance onstage. In addition to the artificial dress, similar to that worn by the other males, he also wears earrings. At his second appearance, as Petruchio "come to wive it wealthily in Padua," he rides a minute and extremely dusty donkey and wears a hat that could have been earned by Lois from the attentions of Mr Harris, plutocrat. Keel's normal macho appearance, reasserted in a year's time in *Seven Brides for Seven Brothers* (1954), is here undermined.[23]

The offcasting missing from the two male leads is to be found, rather, in the parts of the two hoodlums, played by Keenan Wynn and James Whitmore. These are odd crooks. One faints at the mention of cattle-branding; the other has pretensions to be a tap-dancer. They become embroiled in the production, and ham their parts with gusto. Their involvement is such that they adopt a parody Elizabethan language offstage, and misquote from *Hamlet* and *Romeo and Juliet*: "to flee or not to flee," and "going away is such sweet sorrow." Unhappily, their new careers are cut short when their boss is murdered. The IOU no longer has any value and they reluctantly leave to join their new boss, almost forgetting to change out of their stage clothes. Before they go, however, they put on a show to console Fred for the loss of Lilli.

At this point the film changes register. So far it has displayed the Shakespearean "dance of human passions" by parodying them. Now the discords drop away as the film moves towards its closing reconciliation. The change is signalled by a reference to Shakespeare, as one of the hoods tells Fred to:

> Just remember what the immortal bard once said, "all the world's a stage and all the men and women merely players"— unquote.

This time the quotation is precise. It is the opening of Jaques' famous speech in *As You Like It*, and it asserts the universality of drama. It is evidence, too, for the protean nature and "perpetual modernity" of the "classic" author. Kermode and Wittgenstein are therefore vindicated, and in the most inauspicious setting: the back alley behind the theatre.[24]

The song they perform in that setting is, of course, "Brush Up Your Shakespeare," the song with which I began. They perform it to a soft-shoe shuffle, riddled with mistakes but executed with all the zest and self-confidence of a Jimmy Durante. Fred watches, silent and fascinated. After he leaves to prepare for the second Act, the hoods reprise the song directly to the camera. They have now taken the immortal Bard at his word. Previously, most of the onstage production was performed before a theatre audience. Now, by directly addressing the camera the hoods have rendered this surrogate redundant. They have turned the back alley, and ultimately the whole world, into a stage. And, since their performance is closely related to vaudeville, they have turned Shakespeare into a showman.[25]

If Shakespeare is a showman and the whole world's a stage, then he is the master of us all. In another context, the hoods are restating a remark made by Fred to Lilli before she left, that their marriage had been a great "script," and that they had failed to live up to it. The two hoods do their best to live up to the script, and they prepare the way for Lilli's return, in time to give a shortened version of Katherina's final speech:

> I am ashamed that women are so simple
> To offer war where they should kneel for peace.[26]

The misogyny implied in this speech, and which informs much

of *Kiss Me, Kate*, is no longer acceptable to us. There is no doubting, however, the speech's reconciliatory power. It unites the onstage action with the offstage life of Fred and Lilli, and brings the film to an appropriate conclusion.

Because they are the harbingers of that reconciliation, the two hoods join the gallery of Shakespeare's corrupt yet perceptive comic characters. They are similar in kind to Falstaff, and it is worth recalling that Samuel Johnson, after clearly enumerating Falstaff's flaws, concluded that:

> the man thus corrupt, thus despicable, makes himself necessary to the prince that despises him, by the most pleasing of all qualities, perpetual gaiety, by an unfailing power of exciting laughter, which is the more freely indulged, as his wit is not of the splendid or ambitious kind, but consists in easy escapes and sallies of levity, which make sport but raise no envy.[27]

No finer comment can be made about the hoods as they brush up their Shakespeare.

NOTES

1 Cole Porter, *The Complete Lyrics of Cole Porter*, ed. Robert Kimball (London: Hamish Hamilton, 1983), p. 279.

2 I. A. Richards, *Principles of Literary Criticism* (London: Kegan Paul, 1926), p. 36. T. S. Eliot, *Selected Prose*, ed. Frank Kermode (London: Faber and Faber, 1975), p. 174. F. R. Leavis, *Letters in Criticism* (London: Chatto and Windus, 1974), p. 134. A fascinating discussion of the polarization of American culture is to be found in Lawrence W. Levine, *Highbrow/Lowbrow: The Emergence of Cultural Hierarchy in America* (Cambridge, MA: Harvard University Press, 1988).

3 Stanley Kauffmann, *Figures of Light: Film Criticism and Commentary* (New York: Harper and Row, 1971), p. 113. Leo Braudy, *The World in a Frame: What We See in Films* (Garden City, NY: Anchor Press/Doubleday, 1976), pp. 105–9. D. J. Wenden, *The Birth of the Movies* (New York: E. P. Dutton, 1975), p. 36. David Pirie, *Anatomy of the Movies* (London: Windward, 1981), p. 32.

4 Eliot, *Selected Prose*, p. 130.

5 Frank Kermode, "Introduction" to Eliot, *Selected Prose*, pp. 19-21; *The Classic* (London: Faber and Faber, 1975), pp. 38, 75–6; *Forms of Attention* (Chicago: University of Chicago Press, 1985), p. 62.

6 Peter Conrad, "Operatic Shakespeare," *Romantic Opera and Literary Form* (London: University of California Press, 1977), pp. 42–69, particularly pp. 42–3. On the relationship between the Romantics and the Bard, see Jonathan Bate, *Shakespeare and the English Romantic Imagination* (Oxford: Clarendon Press, 1986), p. 6 and passim. On the changing status of Shakespeare in America, see Levine, *Highbrow/Lowbrow*, pp. 13–81.

7 Ludwig Wittgenstein, *Culture and Value*, ed. G. H. Von Wright, trans. Peter Winch (Oxford: Basil Blackwell, 1980), pp. 36–7, 48, 83, 86. Two critics who have been influenced by Wittgenstein are Germaine Greer, in *Shakespeare* (Oxford: OUP, 1986), pp. 40, 67–8, 108; and Terence Hawkes, in *That Shakespeherian Rag* (London: Methuen, 1986), p. vi.

8 Jan Kott, "Hamlet of the Mid-Century," in *Shakespeare our Contemporary*, trans. Boleslaw Taborski (London: Methuen, 1967), pp. 47–60. Charles W. Eckert, "Introduction," *Focus on Shakespearean Films*, ed. Eckert (Englewood Cliffs, NJ: Prentice-Hall, 1972), p. 1. Ian Johnson, "Merely Players," *Focus on Shakespearean Films*, pp. 8–9. Stanley Green, *Broadway Musicals of the 30s* (New York: Da Capo Press, 1971), pp. 106–7, 172–5. Clive Hirschhorn, *The Hollywood Musical* (London: Octopus Books, 1981), pp. 170, 174, 372. Leonard Bernstein, *Bernstein on Broadway* (New York: G. Schirmer, 1981), p. 248. David Pirie, *Anatomy of the Movies* (London: Windward, 1981), p. 254. For an account of the conditions of production and reception of early Shakespeare films, see Roberta E. Pearson and William Uriccio, "How many times shall Caesar bleed in sport: Shakespeare and the cultural debate about moving pictures," *Screen* Vol. 31 No 3 (Autumn 1990), pp. 243–61. A discussion of six films is provided by Peter S. Donaldson, *Shakespearean Films/Shakespearean Directors* (Boston: Unwin Hyman, 1990).
9 Gilbert Seldes, *Movies for the Millions: An Account of Motion Pictures, principally in America* (London: Batsford, 1937), p. 69.
10 Shakespeare, *The Taming of the Shrew* (Harmondsworth, Middlesex: Penguin, 1968), pp. 10, 121. Johnson, "Merely Players," p. 7. Basil Wright, *The Long View: An International History of the Cinema* (London: Paladin, 1976), p. 91. Leslie Halliwell, *Halliwell's Filmgoer's Companion* (7th edn, London: Granada, 1980), p. 716. The credit line is: "Adapted for the Screen and Directed by Sam Taylor," which seems quite innocuous.
11 Julian Mates, *America's Musical Stage: Two Hundred Years of Musical Theatre* (Westport, CT: Greenwood Press, 1985), pp. 137–8. Mark Twain, *The Adventures of Huckleberry Finn* (1884; rpt. Harmondsworth, Middlesex: Penguin, 1966), pp. 197–200, 213–8. Hirschhorn, *The Hollywood Musical*, p. 236. For a discussion of nineteenth-century parodies of just one play, *Hamlet*, see James Ellis, "The Counterfeit Presentment," *Nineteenth Century Theatre Research* 11 No 1 (Summer 1983) pp. 29–50.
12 *Hamlet* I, ii, 1–159 (Harmondsworth, Middlesex: Penguin, 1980), pp. 70–5. Olivier's attitude and chair, in turn, derives from photographs of Edwin Booth as Hamlet. See Levine, *Highbrow/Lowbrow*, p. 51. For some discussion of the Olivier film, see Peter Davison, *Hamlet: Text and Performance* (London: Macmillan, 1983), pp. 47–54.
13 See Patricia Meyer Spacks, *John Gay* (New York: Twayne Publishers, Inc., 1965), pp. 122–5.
14 Michael B. Druxman, *The Musical: From Broadway to Hollywood* (London: Thomas Yoseloff, 1980), p. 47. Alain Masson, "George Sidney: Artificial Brilliance/The Brilliance of Artifice," *Genre: The Musical*, ed. Rick Altman (London: Routledge & Kegan Paul, 1981), p. 33. On Olivier's *Henry V* see Harry Geduld, *Filmguide to Henry V* (Bloomington: Indiana University Press, 1973), pp. 24–25, 67. For one assessment of the impact of Olivier's *Henry V*, see Robert Brustein, "Once More Into the Breach," *The New Republic* 9 November 1986, p. 28.
15 Porter, *The Complete Lyrics*, p. 277.
16 John Kobal, *Rita Hayworth: The Time, the Place and the Woman* (London: W. H. Allen, 1977), pp. 138–41, 198–218; *Gotta Sing Gotta Dance: A Pictorial History of the Musicals* (London: Hamlyn, 1970), pp. 273–7. Obituary of Rita Hayworth, *The Times* (London) 16 May 1987, pp. 20, 22. Harry S. Truman, *Year of Decisions, 1945* (London: Hodder & Stoughton, 1955), p. 352. See also Richard F. Haynes, *The Awesome Power: Harry S. Truman as Commander-in-Chief* (Baton Rouge: Louisiana State University Press, 1973), p. 55. On Cyd Charisse, see Dennis Giles, "Show-Making," *Genre: The Musical*, ed. Altman, pp. 85–101.
17 The most important text on the backstage musical is Jane Feuer, *The Hollywood Musical* (2nd ed., London: Macmillan, 1993).
18 On the influence of the Quattrocento on the Elizabethan stage, see E. K. Chambers, *The Elizabethan Stage* (4 vols, Oxford: Clarendon Press, 1923), III, pp. 9-13. On Mannerism, see Walter Friedlaender, *Mannerism and Anti-Mannerism in Italian Painting* (NYC: Schocken Books, 1965), particularly pp. 3–5, 10–11, 38; and David Rosand, "Theater and Structure in the Art of Paolo Veronese," *Art Bulletin* 55 (June 1973) pp. 217–39, particu-

larly 225. I am grateful to John Gash of the Department of History of Art, Aberdeen University, for drawing the Pontormo and Parmigianino paintings to my attention. On some of the pictorial debts of *Henry V*, see Geduld, *Filmguide to Henry V*, pp. 18–19, 46, 58–63.

19 *The Taming of the Shrew* I, ii, 74 and IV, i, 126; Penguin pp. 77, 119. Porter, *Complete Lyrics*, pp. 275–6, 278. The lyrics have been altered slightly for the film, and include the reference to *Citizen Kane*. Feuer, *The Hollywood Musical*, pp. 1, 3, 18, 27–30, 47.

20 Cathy Klaprat, "The Star as Market Stategy: Bette Davis in Another Light," *The American Film Industry*, ed. Tino Balio (rev. ed., Madison: University of Wisconsin Press, 1985), pp. 372–5.

21 Delamater, *Dance in the Hollywood Musical*, p. 78. Kobal, *Gotta Sing Gotta Dance*, pp. 262–3, 266. Porter, *Complete Lyrics*, p. 278. *Taming of the Shrew*, I, i, 153, Penguin pp. 70–1. On *Easter Parade*, see Bruce Babington and Peter William Evans, *Blue Skies and Silver Linings: Aspects of the Hollywood Musical* (Manchester: Manchester University Press, 1985), Ch. 2. On Miller in *On The Town*, see Richard Dyer, "Entertainment and Utopia"; and for a brief note on Sidney's miscasting, see Masson, "George Sidney," both in *Genre: The Musical*, ed. Altman, pp. 31–2, 188–9.

22 *The Taming of the Shrew*, I, ii, 88–91, Penguin p. 78. Kobal, *Gotta Sing Gotta Dance*, pp. 260–1, 264–6.

23 I am grateful to my students, Eve John and Judith Worrall, for these points. On changes in the status of women in Elizabethan England, see G. R. Hibbard's "Introduction" to the Penguin edition of *The Taming of the Shrew*, pp. 16–17, 29–35. On changes in the status of women in postwar America, see William H. Chafe, *Women and Equality: Changing Patterns in American Culture* (New York: Oxford University Press, 1977), pp. 92–108.

24 Druxman, *The Musical*, p. 47. *As You Like It* (Harmondsworth, Middlesex: Penguin, 1968), I, vii, 140–1, p. 87.

25 The same effect occurs, briefly, in the opening sequence of Minelli's *Ziegfeld Follies*, when Shakespeare is compared to P. T. Barnum and Florenz Ziegfeld.

26 *The Taming of the Shrew*, V, ii, 160–1, Penguin p. 155.

27 Samuel Johnson, "Notes on *2 Henry IV*," *Johnson on Shakespeare*, ed. Arthur Sherbo (2 vols, New Haven, CT: Yale University Press, 1968), I, p. 523.

8

Who Loves You Porgy?
The Debates Surrounding
Gershwin's Musical

David Horn

In 1989 the Royal Liverpool Philharmonic Society planned two
performances of *Porgy and Bess*: one a conventional concert
performance, the other a "community" performance, in which
part of the audience, drawn from the area in which the
Philharmonic Hall stands (a city centre area with a high proportion of elderly and people on low incomes), would join with
the Society's choir in "six or eight selected passages of suitable,
familiar or exciting material."[1] Rehearsals were to be held in
the weeks before at suitable local venues. The object was to
encourage greater involvement by the local community,
including its Black population, in the activities at the Hall.
Opposition to the idea was expressed in strong terms by a local
Black arts organization, the Liverpool Anti-Racist and
Community Arts Association (LARCAA), on the grounds that the
work's depiction of Black people would give offence and would
be likely to reinforce existing prejudices. Surprised by the vehe-
mence of the attack, the Society countered with arguments
which spoke of *Porgy and Bess* being about "the triumph of the
spirit" and Gershwin's attempts to forge an integrated
"American idiom" out of the various racial, religious, and cultural materials available to him. LARCAA were not persuaded

by these arguments and maintained their opposition to the community performance, suggesting in addition that a booklet, "The Truth About *Porgy and Bess*" be produced for distribution to the audience at the concert performance. A little over two months before it was due to take place, the Society cancelled the community performance.

*   *   *

Commentators on *Porgy and Bess* have frequently felt obliged to make reference to "controversies" which have arisen in its wake. Some have looked beyond controversies and have perceived ambiguities and contradictions, both in the work and in its reception. In what was the first sustained attempt at analysis, British musicologist Wilfrid Mellers saw tensions as inherent—for example, between the innocence of spirit of the folk community and the threat of corruption through urban sophistication. For Mellers, these tensions are part of the work's artistic strength and, ultimately, of its unity. This view permits him to make a rounded interpretation of the work as being "about the impact of the world of commerce on those who once led, who would like to have led, may still lead, the 'good life', based on a close relationship between man and nature."[2]

American musicologist Richard Crawford, by contrast, focussed attention on tensions between interpretive positions:

> *Porgy and Bess* ... has symbolized different things to different men [sic] as forcibly as any other American musical work that comes to mind.[3]

Crawford identified four "perspectives": *Porgy and Bess* as opera; as American folklore; as racial stereotype; and as cultural exploitation. His position is unusual in musicology in that it allows for a plurality of interpretation. In this essay I wish to develop this basic approach by identifying what I suggest are two debates about *Porgy and Bess*, the "artistic" debate and the "race" debate. Within each of these a diversity of interpretive positions have been assumed, often in tension with one another. But I also suggest that the two debates have rarely if ever, connected, and that this leads to something of an impasse. After analyzing the two debates I wish to argue that it is possible to set up a dialogue between them and that this could permit alternative readings to be made. At that point, however, we must allow the specific circumstances of the Liverpool episode to have another word.

The Two Debates

The artistic debate has revolved around one central question: is *Porgy and Bess* an opera? The issue was raised by first night critics in 1935. "The style is at one moment of opera and another of operetta or sheer Broadway entertainment," wrote *New York Times* critic Olin Downes.[4] The arrival in the opera house of a "popular" songwriter clearly ruffled many feathers, including those of composer Virgil Thomson. Thomson had an interest in the government-funded Federal Music Project, and was consequently anxious not to seem anti-populist. Yet at the same time he was keen to defend the uniqueness of "serious" music, and he identified as a basic weakness what, in his view, was the ambiguous position of Gershwin and the work:

> [Gershwin] hasn't learned the business of being a serious composer ... I don't mind his being a light composer and I don't mind his trying to be a serious one. But I do mind his falling between two stools.[5]

Theatrical producers and drama critics have often been impatient with this argument. Looking back on the original 1935 production, its director Reuben Mamoulian commented, "Critics at the time complained it wasn't an opera and it wasn't a musical. You give someone something delicious to eat and they complain because they have no name for it."[6]

Despite such scorn, and despite the accusation that prejudice against popular culture was the real source of the argument, the debate has persisted. When musicologist Lawrence Starr attended the 1977 Houston Grand Opera production, he went, he tells us, with "limited expectations ... expecting to hear a group of splendid show tunes, loosely strung together..." But instead, he said, "I had a most profound surprise—profound in every sense of the word. Of course I saw an *opera*."[7] The point, for our present purposes, is not Starr's conversion and the

111

reasons for it, but that he felt the need to set his reevaluation in the context of the opera-musical debate, almost fifty years after the issue was first raised.

Why has the question of the status of *Porgy and Bess* been so persistent? The history of the argument suggests that there are two principal reasons. Both are connected to a particular view of the nature and function of opera. The first reason has to do with artistic integration and unity, the second with a concept of opera as able to give expression to fundamental human feelings (hence, perhaps, Starr's phrase, "profound in every sense of the word").

Prior to Mellers' analysis in 1964, the prevailing view among those music critics and scholars who bothered to take notice of *Porgy and Bess* seems to have been that the kind of compositional unity found in much grand opera was lacking in this case. Significantly, the 1942 Cheryl Crawford production, which dropped the recitatives, was judged by some to be:

> a far more unified whole ... the action and the accompanying score had been tightened; they did not have a chance to wander from their main course, and as a consequence the song-hits became an integral part of the drama.[8]

When Mellers speaks of "the relationship of parts to whole" as demonstrating "a genuine musical–dramatic integration," the integration he has in mind is of a different order. He shows, for example, how the key of B flat links Porgy and Bess's love duet with Sportin' Life's "marvellously seductive" song, "There's a Boat Dat's Leavin' Soon For New York"; how the music of Crown's triumph over Bess on Kittiwah Island is "unmistakeably related" to Porgy's recurring theme.[9]

The clearest exposition of the argument that *Porgy and Bess* displays genuine operatic unity is in the essay by Starr. Starr speaks of "a wealth of unifying devices" operating on both musical and dramatic levels:

> These range from numerous "reminiscence themes" to substantial harmonic and thematic designs which can unite entire scenes or create marked interrelationships between scenes. One also finds considerable use of leitmotivs

112

throughout the score, involving much motivic development in the orchestral parts.

Starr reserves a place in his essay for the vexed question of recitatives. This was a feature which drama critics had found especially problematic in 1935. *New York Times* drama critic Brooks Atkinson had asked "why commonplace remarks that carry no emotion have to be made in a chanting monotone," resulting in a "deluge of remarks ... that annoyingly impeded the action." Starr's analysis, by contrast, discovered

> little jewels of melody ... on virtually every page of the score. Much of the recitative was shown to consist of short lyrical phrases, bordering on *arioso*, that are completely of a piece with the melodic and rhythmic language of the songs in the opera.

He then makes an important addition:

> It is as if the recitative in the opera is *potential* song, a musical language that grows into song with considerable ease and smoothness whenever the drama renders it appropriate or necessary.[10]

The second reason for the persistence of arguments about *Porgy and Bess* as opera, that of the operatic stage as the setting for the exploration of the human condition, moves us away from the formal into the social arena, and the two debates, the artistic debate and the race debate, have the opportunity to connect. In the event, however, they do so only for the validity of the connection to be denied.

Mellers and Starr, both strong apologists for *Porgy and Bess*, make the point that, in their view, the work is about the human, not the Black American, condition. "The theme," in Mellers' words, "applies, obviously, to urban, industrialized man whatever the colour of his skin: the plight of the Negro merely gives peculiarly pointed manifestation, because the contrast between his innocence and urban sophistication is acute." Starr seems to want to direct his remarks at a particular audience:

> Opera, after all, is *not* sociology or cultural history; it is dramatic theater.... It is best simply to say that *Porgy and Bess* is

an opera about human beings, who in this particular story
happen to be black.... To insist on viewing *Porgy and Bess* as
a racial document is to apply criteria which lie wholly outside
the tradition to which this work relates...[11]

Starr, then, is aware of another debate, that of *Porgy and Bess*
as "racial document," but the primacy of musico-dramatic evidence, in his view, causes him to regard any other kind as inap-
propriate. This musico-dramatic evidence points to an
interpretation which, at bottom, vindicates a view of art as able
to cut through to humanity's heart and not be ensnared in the
confusion of surface contexts. Mellers' reading has much in
common with this, except that he sees the story in general as a
parable of the human spirit confronted by the particular problems of being human in the twentieth century.

Although neither writer engages with this other debate, there
is a hint in Starr's words ("to insist on...") that he is aware of the
strength of feeling that fuels it. That strength of feeling was
apparent from an early stage in the reception of the work, and
although, like the artistic debate, the race debate has been conducted at best fitfully, its frequent outspokenness makes it surprising that it can, if desired, simply be ignored. The hurt which
many have felt is epitomized by Tim Dennison:

Perhaps, the secret of [*Porgy and Bess*'s] success is that it is
earthy, sexy, corrupt, violent, comical, irreligious, blasphe-
mous, hypocritical, desecrating to the spirituals, immoral,
and altogether derogatory to the American Negro...[12]

Like the artistic debate, the race debate arises from one basic
question. The problem addressed here, however, has nothing to
do with concern over operatic status and what that implies, but
rather with the question: does this work by three white
Americans prejudice the interests of Black Americans? All the
intricacies of the argument appear to follow from this, and
while some commentators have sought to widen the basic question beyond *Porgy and Bess*, seeing it as symbolic of a deeper
problem, it is noticeable that most discussion arises from the
specificity of the work itself and its production history.

An overview of the debate suggests the existence of four main

themes: Black America as subject; stereotyping in characterization and dialect; Gershwin's version of Black musical idioms; and
performers. The argument over the first of these took on a particular sharpness in 1952, when the State Department announced
its support for a European tour of the Robert Breen production,
including an appearance in Moscow. While performances had
been confined to the United States, critics of the work's depiction
of Southern Black life had been confronted by the argument,
amongst others, that American audiences had sufficient knowledge to make adjustments. The possibility that European audiences would be unable to do the same permitted critics to restate
the argument that *Porgy and Bess* was an unacceptable portrait.
In this view they found unlikely allies in those Congressmen who
feared the propaganda Communists might make from evidence
of squalor and oppression among America's Black population. In
the event, little proof could be found to show that European audiences did view *Porgy and Bess* this way. William Warfield, who
played Porgy, had considerable reservations about singing "I Got
Plenty o' Nuttin'," but of the tour itself he commented:

> [European audiences] had an intelligent understanding of
> the real situation in America, and loved the show for its real
> qualities.[13]

The announcement in 1956 of a movie version of *Porgy and
Bess* occasioned a renewed attack on the work's depiction of
Black life. Black singers and actors were strongly advised by
an advertisement in the *Hollywood Reporter* not to get involved
in portraying:

> Negroes ... [as] given to erupting with all sorts of goings-on
> after their day's work in the white folks' kitchen or the white
> folks' yard was over, like sniffing happy dust, careless love,
> crapshooting, drinking, topping it all off with knife play.

The unknown writer goes on to insist that *Porgy and Bess* suggests such behavior is innate, and to offer the alternative perspective that "this was a human being's way of reacting to the
dehumanizing power of a master race."[14]
As we have seen, those more concerned with the artistic

115

debate largely ignored this issue. Among those who recognised that it required a response, the main tactic was to challenge the implied synecdoche: there was no reason why this particular part (of Black life) should be taken to represent the whole. Harold Cruse's retort to this line of reasoning was to reassert, in vehement terms, that racial politics—including the racial politics of art—was the fundamental issue:

> The fact that such Negro types *did* exist is beside the point. Culturally, it is a product of American developments that were intended to shunt Negroes off into a tight box of sub-cultural, artistic dependence, stunted growth, caricature, aesthetic self-mimicry imposed by others, and creative insolvency.[15]

On rare occasions, a positive view of the work was put forward which recognized the problem inherent in white Americans creating a portrait of Blacks and went on from there to praise the result. One such was British theater critic Kenneth Tynan who wrote, after seeing the touring production in London in 1953, that *Porgy and Bess* "remains the fullest exploration of the Negro mind any white man has ever made."[16]

To a considerable extent, the second theme—that of stereotyping—has crystallized the broader arguments about the portrait of Black life. At the level of language, the type of dialect used has given rise to accusations of minstrelization. But the main debate has centred around characterization. In the context of a richly-detailed account of the ways in which Blacks have been portrayed in American song, Sam Dennison comments of *Porgy and Bess*:

> In spite of the best of intentions, Gershwin perpetrated stereotypes in music the same way that well-meaning Harriet Beecher Stowe had done.... The "happy darky" Porgy cheerfully emulates Uncle Tom with his "I got plenty o' nuttin'."[17]

Outside the racial debate, the particular charge of which this is one example is implicitly challenged by writers such as Starr, who point to the artistic skills which result in a depth of characterization. In doing so, however, as we have seen, they deny the admissibility of the racial argument. The problem is that what may be accepted artistically may still give offence socially and politically unless the specifics of this particular society, its time and place are acknowledged. The dilemma is particularly sharp for performers, as can be seen in comments made by William Warfield. Warfield is responding to those who charged performers with "Uncle-Tomming":

> ... those of us in *Porgy and Bess* saw ourselves as playing only roles, and in no way did we play them as black ordinary stereotypes. It was art, and we were artists. At the same time I have to say there was a fine line as far as my own sympathies were concerned; I could agree with the need for blacks to play roles that would provide more respect.

Warfield opts for justification by art, but this leaves him uncertain vis-à-vis the social and political question. By contrast, another performer, Clamma Dale, who played Bess in the 1977 Houston Grand Opera production, attempts to face up to the accusation of offensively stereotyped characters on its own social and political ground and to seek justification there. Impatient with what she terms the "fist-shaking honky-calling" view of Bess, she offers the opinion that Bess has to be understood first and foremost as a Black woman:

> She's extremely vulnerable, but has somehow, as most black women have always had, an ability to survive. My silent script for her is that she had to leave home, she had to survive, had to hustle, not just as a prostitute, but hustle the way I do as an artist—doing church jobs, temple jobs, children's jobs—to keep herself together.[18]

The issue of Gershwin's use of identifiable Black musical idioms is one, we might expect, to be addressed in both debates, but from a different perspective. In the artistic debate, indeed, the question has to do with arguments over stylistic integrity (Mellers is particularly good at linking it into his broader theme). In the race debate it seems likely, therefore, that it will have to do with the politics of appropriation. In broad terms, this is so, but the topic is not dealt with in any detail. Duke Ellington complained of Gershwin's "lampblack Negroisms" (he later changed his opinion), and jazz historian Rudi Blesh characterized the music as "Negroesque." By contrast, J. Rosamond Johnson, who played Lawyer Frazier in the first production, praised Gershwin to his face for being "the Abraham Lincoln of Negro music." None of these specified what they meant, or discussed the implications. Black musician and writer Hall Johnson's detailed assessment focussed, when it came to the music itself, on the gap he perceived between what Gershwin had given his characters to sing, and what such people would and could have sung in reality.[19]

A detail in the history of the composition of *Porgy and Bess* is relevant here, for it indicates that the question of appropriation had exercised the mind of at least one of its creators. Recalling Gershwin's visit to Folly Island, near Charleston, in 1934, DuBose Heyward (librettist and author of the original, 1925, novel), described what he saw as Gershwin's profound affinity for Black music:

> ...the most interesting discovery to me, as we sat listening to their spirituals, or watched a group shuffling before a cabin or country store, was that to George it was more like a homecoming than an exploration.[20]

As Richard Crawford has observed, Heyward's account of how Gershwin attended a prayer meeting featuring the practice of "shouting" and "stole the show from their champion shouter," "may be an ethnocentric judgement," but Heyward's comments, published in 1935, may have effectively defused the argument, by insisting on Gershwin's deep affection for, and affiliation to Black music. Tim Dennison does not deny this, and is reduced to asserting that "living in close contact with the Negro, attending their meetings, singing, shouting with, watching and listening to them" was "something a Negro composer would not have to do." Cruse's view concurs with that of Dennison, but goes one step further, pulling the debate back into the political and economic arena:

> ...such a folk-opera, even if it *had been written* by Negroes, would never have been supported, glorified and acclaimed, as *Porgy* has, by the white cultural elite of America.[21]

We have seen that the position of the Black cast of *Porgy and Bess* occasioned opposing comment. Cruse provides the most outspoken example of one side of the argument:

> ...the folk-opera *Porgy and Bess* should be forever banned by all Negro performers in the United States. No Negro singer, actor, or performer should ever submit to a role in this vehicle again. If white producers want to stage this folk-opera it should be performed by white performers made up in blackface, because it is distorted imitation all the way through.[22]

Black performers themselves have sometimes confessed to mixed emotions at performing in *Porgy and Bess*, and at least one was evidently subjected to pressure.[23] For some performers, reservations about the work were overcome by the sheer quality of the cast, but for Maya Angelou, who was a dancer in the company during the European tour in 1952-3, both the work and the performers made a deep impact. Although she expected the initial effect of the show to wear off, "over the next year ... I found myself more touched by the tale and more and more impressed by the singers who told it."[24]

These various positions in the race debate arose out of the basic problematic of a work by white Americans about Blacks. Remarkably few commentators have seen fit to introduce the subject of the particular ethnicity of two of the three authors. For instance, Charles Schwartz, in an Appendix to his biography of Gershwin, points to what he calls "Jewishisms" in Gershwin's music, including three examples from *Porgy and Bess* of a partiality for minor thirds. Yet when assessing the work itself, Schwartz prefers the arguments of those who:

> ...question not only the Uncle Tomisms in the opera but the underlying conceit of the work—that Gershwin could set himself up as a musical spokesman for the blacks represented in *Porgy and Bess*.[25]

Isaac Goldberg, Gershwin's acquaintance and first biographer, thought that a musical connection could be made between the two ethnic minorities. He pointed out that Gershwin became "increasingly conscious of the similarity between the folk song

119

of the Negro and of the Polish [Jewish] pietists." But he left it to others to explore the matter further. Thirty-five years later, Wilfrid Mellers made a broad sociological connection:

> George Gershwin was not, like Porgy, a Negro, nor, in the material benefits of life, was he in any way deprived. He was, however, a poor boy who made good: an American Jew who knew all about spiritual isolation and, in Tin Pan Alley, had opportunity enough to learn about corruption.[26]

The sparse literature on ethnicity and music in the United States contains numerous hints that the question of a musical dialogue between Jews and African-Americans deserves closer scrutiny. At the same time, cultural historians Lewis Erenberg and Berndt Ostendorf have both pointed to a parallel socio-cultural dialogue.[27] But no one seems yet to have examined in any depth the link between the two.

The Musicality of Catfish Row

On one apparently simple thing the two debates agree: *Porgy and Bess* is an artistic work for the musical stage, which uses a group of Black Americans as its subject matter. The order is important. From the positive artistic perspective it permits the view that the Black American world portrayed by the authors is not racial but symbolically human. From the hostile side of the race debate perspective, the order permits the view that one culture's (bourgeois) art conventions are seen to dominate the harsh reality of another culture's social deprivation and to exploit its expressivity. In both cases the issue has to do with an acceptance of the authors' creative control: the world they portray is manipulated by them.

But neither position allows for the paradox through which so much of the theatre works, the suspension of disbelief by means of which what we know to be someone's creation appears as an autonomous world, in which those involved are responsible for what occurs. Accepting the autonomy of Catfish Row as a starting point in this way has one immediate effect. It means the question of specificity is no longer in doubt. The action takes place between particular people in a particular

place at a particular time. We may choose to view them symbolically if we wish, but they are themselves and do not have to
stand for anything.

That this specific community is distinguished by race is, of
course, visually apparent from the start. But the full significance of this emerges for the first time after the murder of
Robbins, when a white detective appears. This has two effects:
it underlines the racially distinctive nature of Catfish Row, and
it suggests that the community is socially circumscribed. On
top of that, something else happens which, I suggest, plays on
our acceptance of the illusion of autonomy. The white detective's part is spoken, and it is plain speech, flat and dull. Up to
now, the people of Catfish Row have sung all the time. The
closest they come to speech is infused with inflections and
rhythms of song. The white detective's speech makes me
realize that what I had taken to be convention—people sing in
operas—is more than that. In contrast to the external white
community, Catfish Row expresses itself in song. This realiza-
tion depends on my being aware that I have accepted an illusion, but more important, it could not occur had I not accepted
it. What is happening is an inversion of the order of priorities
we noted earlier. The particular nature of Catfish Row recon-
structs how I think of opera. Instead of an artistic conceit by
means of which one group of people causes another, imagined,
group to conduct their lives to music in order in some way
to get at their souls, the people of Catfish Row reveal the
musicality of their daily life.

Once revealed, this musicality shows itself to be complex and
varied. The people draw on a range of styles and approaches:
collective religious expression, and religious expression in
which individual and group are integrated; songs about work,
again involving individual and group; solo songs with accompaniment; romantic duets; jazz-influenced singing about life in
the city, and so on. The author-centred perspective on this produces several unreconcilable positions: Gershwin as unsuc-
cessfully eclectic; as poorly imitative of Black culture; as
exploiting Black culture; as achieving an integration which
reflects that of the American social ideal. But if we start from
the point of the autonomy and specificity of Catfish Row, what

121

from one perspective might seem eclecticism becomes the creative drawing by the community on sedimented layers of music, built up over a period of time—some very old, some very new. The idea of exploitation seems irrelevant—Catfish Row cannot exploit itself—as indeed does that of integration. What happens is that material from these sedimented layers is used by the people of Catfish Row to negotiate the relationships between concepts fundamental to their lives and to changes in those lives—between, for example, sacred and secular, male and female, urban and rural, old and new.

Perhaps the most basic of all the relationships is that between public and private. What occurs on Catfish Row and on Kittiwah Island revolves around dramatic conflicts between individuals, but it is evident that everything that happens is both an individual and a communal experience. The community is not a commentator, or merely a foil, it is actively affected and affecting (as, for example in the hurricane scene). On a more subtle level, in the mourning scene following Robbins's death, public prayer and private sorrow are interdependent.

It is noticeable that on Catfish Row there is no wholly private expression. Individual utterances take place in the presence of—and often with the help of—the community in one form or another. When two people escape the community (as do Crown and Bess on Kittiwah Island) the consequences threaten not just them but the community itself. It is also noticeable that, at times of individual crisis, the community influence can be crucial. When Bess is delirious, her cure is in some way assisted by the traditional calling of the street vendors. Individuals, in their turn, can use public music for private aspirations: at the end of the story, Porgy adapts ideas and images from the spirituals to apply to his hope to follow Bess to New York.

We begin to see communal music as providing the bedrock for Catfish Row. Individuals can be integrated into it, without losing their individuality, or they may draw on more recent layers of sedimented expression to express alternative ideas. Crown's "Red Headed Woman" hurricane song, provocatively dedicated to his "Big Frien" (God), opposes the community's frightened prayerfulness with an assertion of prowess couched in rough-and-ready dancehall music. More subtle responses

122

are also possible. Porgy and Bess express their love, which scandalizes the community and begins a process of separation for Porgy, in an idiom which draws heavily on romantic operatic song. From the author-centred perspective within the race debate, this choice of idiom is an alien imposition by Gershwin, but seen from the autonomous perspective of Catfish Row it suggests that Porgy and Bess feel, for whatever reason, they have to look outside their culture for a new framework for their feelings. But they do not simply appropriate the European, individual-centred idiom. Porgy begins the melody of their song ("Bess, You Is My Woman Now") with the expectation of a long high line, but shifts it immediately to a lower, slightly syncopated one, in which, on the first syllable of "wo-man", there is a "blue note." The community's own resources are not only being adapted in new circumstances, they are being used to reconstruct imported ones.

The intricate musicality of Catfish Row permits many subtleties of relationship to be explored. Sportin' Life is often the root of the accusation of stereotyping, but if we accept his autonomy, we can see an example of this subtlety at work. On the one hand, his choice of idiom sets him aside from the rest, and the way he mocks the community's naive religiosity ("It Ain't Necessarily So") appears to confirm this. On the other hand, he shares with others—and especially with Porgy—the ability to fashion melody out of the rhythms and cadences of ordinary speech. A good example is his first attempt to lure Bess away to New York, while the rest of Catfish Row is preparing for the picnic—"Picnics is all right for these small town suckers..."[28]

This may be one of the "little jewels of melody" which excited Lawrence Starr. Starr viewed them as an example of Gershwin's achievement in creating a unified work. I am suggesting that Sportin' Life's inventive approach to melody, here and elsewhere in the story, shows his own creativity at work, one based on individualism. Other kinds are at work also. The story begins with an example of how, on Catfish Row, public and private are creatively linked. In the first moments, as the people of Catfish Row begin to reveal their world, they sing riff-like, wordless chants. Clara then begins her "Summertime" song, marking the first point at which an individual person draws our gaze. That Clara's individuality is embedded in the community is immediately clear: she sings a lullaby—a personal, private song by a mother for her child—but sings it in a highly public place. Not only that, the first melodic phrase ("Summertime"), emerges out of one of the wordless "doo-oo-da" riffs. Clara's creative motherhood fashions expression out of what she sees and hears around her; from this her baby will one day take strength, as she says, to spread its wings and "take the sky."[29]

*   *   *

The episode in Liverpool, with which I began this essay, introduced the notions of controversy and of different interpretive stances on *Porgy and Bess*. We have explored these positions in some detail within two basic debates, and have also seen how—as was the case in Liverpool when the artistic and race perspectives collided—there has been little or no shared ground on which discussion could take place. But it seems to me the episode in Liverpool has more to say than merely offering contemporary support for a pluralist thesis. Indeed, it could be understood as pointing to a very different viewpoint, namely that in certain specific local circumstances some interpretive positions become hard to maintain.

The hostile reaction expressed by the Black arts organisation LARCAA to the idea of a community performance may well have had its roots in an awareness of a history of Black unease about the work, but there were particular additional factors. When the proposal was made the city was the subject of a council-commissioned investigation, chaired by the socialist peer Lord Gifford, into its race relations. Racism in the city had long been a source of anger, but was now being given new publicity.[30] Particular attention was being focussed on the extent to which both public and private employers had excluded Blacks from employment opportunities. In such circumstances the offer by the Society to begin to repair its longstanding neglect of the local (partly Black) community with a work—however famous and well-loved—by well-to-do white authors about underprivileged Blacks could be regarded as insensitive. It is not hard to see why the Society's defense of its offer on the grounds of the autonomy of art and/or its universal human significance not only cut no ice, but was regarded as supporting the racial *status quo*. From this point of view the critical nature of racial politics in the city meant that in the debate between art and politics it was necessary to insist that *Porgy and Bess* could not be removed from the specifics of the local context, and, in the final analysis, that the politics was more important than the art.

In these circumstances it would be an academic conceit to pretend that promoting the notion of the musical creativity of Catfish Row would have been any more appropriate. But, in another situation, linking it to the idea of a participatory performance of the kind proposed in Liverpool might offer a way forward; not participation in an idealized event, but in one where the racially specific nature of the work was acknowledged, and where the issues could actually be debated. From that base the act of participation in the intricate musicality of Catfish Row could become empowering.

NOTES

1 Information on the Society's concept of the community performance is drawn from an internal document, "Porgy and Bess Community Project for Liverpool", compiled by Phil Thomas, Community/Outreach Worker at the Royal Liverpool Philharmonic Society. I am grateful to Phil Thomas for allowing me to see papers relating to the community performance proposal. All opinions, implicit or otherwise, in this essay, are mine. The episode deserves a fuller account than I have been able to give it here. I have made an initial attempt to do this in "Catfish Row to Granby Street," unpublished paper, Seventh International Conference on Popular Music, Stockton, California, July 1993.
2 Wilfrid Mellers, *Music in a New Found Land: Themes and Developments in the History of American Music* (London: Barrie & Rockliff, 1964), p. 393.
3 Richard Crawford, "It Ain't Necessarily Soul: Gershwin's 'Porgy and Bess' as a Symbol," *Yearbook of Inter American Musical Research* (1972), p. 23.
4 Olin Downes, quoted in Charles Schwartz, *Gershwin: His Life and Music* (Indianapolis: Bobbs-Merrill, 1973), p. 265.
5 Virgil Thomson, quoted in Crawford, "It Ain't Necessarily Soul: Gershwin's 'Porgy and Bess' as a Symbol," p. 25.
6 Reuben Mamoulian, quoted in Hollis Alpert, *The Life and Times of Porgy and Bess: the Story of an American Classic* (New York: Knopf, 1990), p. 322.
7 Lawrence Starr, "Toward a Reevaluation of Gershwin's *Porgy and Bess*", *American Music* Vol. 2 No. 2 (Summer 1984), p. 25. Starr's emphasis.
8 John Tasker Howard, *Our American Music: Three Hundred Years of It* (3rd ed, New York: Crowell, 1954), p. 452.
9 Mellers, *Music in a New Found Land*, pp. 413, 410, 406.
10 Brooks Atkinson, quoted in Schwartz, *Gershwin*, p. 265. Starr, "Toward a Revaluation of Gershwin's *Porgy and Bess*," pp. 29, 33. Starr's emphasis.

11 Mellers, *Music in a New Found Land*, p. 393. Starr, "Toward a Revaluation of *Porgy and Bess*, pp. 26–7. Starr's emphases.

12 Tim Dennison, *The American Negro And His Amazing Music* (New York: Vantage Press, 1963), p. 47.

13 Alpert, *The Life and Times of Porgy and Bess*, pp. 180, 183.

14 Alpert, *The Life and Times of Porgy and Bess*, pp. 260–1.

15 Harold Cruse, *The Crisis of the Negro Intellectual* (New York: William Morrow & Co., 1967), p. 104. Cruse's emphasis.

16 Alpert, *The Life and Times of Porgy and Bess*, p. 177.

17 Sam Dennison, *Scandalize My Name: Black Imagery in American Popular Music* (New York: Garland Publishing, 1982), p. 472.

18 Alpert, *The Life and Times of Porgy and Bess*, pp. 183, 305.

19 Duke Ellington, J. Rosamond Johnson and Hall Johnson, quoted in Alpert, *The Life and Times of Porgy and Bess*, pp. 111, 121, 122. Rudi Blesh, *Shining Trumpets: A History of Jazz* (2nd ed., New York: Knopf, 1958), p. 205.

20 DuBose Heyward, quoted in Edward Jablonski, *Gershwin* (New York: Simon & Schuster, 1988), p. 273.

21 Richard Crawford, "It Ain't Necessarily Soul," p. 21. Dennison, *The American Negro And His Amazing Music*, p.46. Cruse, *The Crisis of the Negro Intellectual*, p. 102.

22 Cruse, *The Crisis of the Negro Intellectual*, p. 103.

23 Sidney Poitier's initial response to being offered the role of Porgy in the screen version was negative, but, according to Hollis Alpert, "pressure on Poitier came from both blacks and whites, undoubtedly stimulated by [Sam] Goldwyn's press agents." See Alpert, *The Life and Times of Porgy and Bess*, p. 261.

24 Maya Angelou, *Singin' and Swingin' and Gettin' Merry Like Christmas* (London: Virago, 1985), p. 166.

25 Charles Schwartz, *Gershwin*, pp. 271, 322–6.

26 Isaac Goldberg, *George Gershwin: A Study in American Music* (1931; rpt. New York: Frederick Ungar Publishing Co., 1958), p. 41. Mellers, *Music in a New Found Land*, p. 392.

27 Lewis Erenberg, *Steppin' Out: New York Night Life and the Transformation of American Culture, 1890–1930* (Chicago: University of Chicago Press, 1984). Berndt Ostendorf, *Ethnicity and Popular Music* (IASPM/UK Working Papers, 2) (Exeter: IASPM/UK, n.d.).

28 George Gershwin, *Porgy and Bess; Vocal Score* (London: Chappell, 1935), pp. 244–5.

29 Gershwin, *Porgy and Bess: Vocal Score*, pp. 7–15.

30 The Gifford report was published in 1989 under the title *Loosen the Shackles: First Report of the Liverpool 8 Inquiry Into Race Relations in Liverpool* (London: Kania Press).

9

West Side Story Revisited

Wilfrid Mellers

Over half a century ago George Gershwin proved, in *Porgy and Bess*, that Broadway need not efface, though it inevitably threatened, the human values we hope to live by. *Porgy* implied an awareness of the modern world such as dream manufacturers, even those as talented as Jerome Kern or Irving Berlin, usually dispensed with. Gershwin's intuitive intelligence was an aspect of his genius; he may not have consciously known that his opera was about the menace that commercialized technocracy offered to the "quality of life." Since 1935, when *Porgy* was first produced, only one popular music-theatre piece has approached its pertinence. *West Side Story* was also the creation of a New York Jew, Leonard Bernstein, who made his substantial living not, like Gershwin, in the commercial theater, but mainly in art and concert music, and as a conductor rather than composer. He owed his success to prodigious talents as composer, conductor, and pianist; yet at the same time he had at least one foot in the commercial world, for no creative and interpretive musician has today been more "fabulously" successful, not merely as a bonafide musician, but also as a charismatic pop composer, media-educator, and TV personality. Informing these multifarious activities was the razor-edge acuity of his mind. Though the original notion of *West Side Story* wasn't his, he immediately understood its potential.

    This didn't mean that the project was rapidly or easily accomplished. It was early in 1949 that Jerome Robbins, a choreographer with a genius to match the composer's, rang Bernstein up to suggest that they might make a modern musical version of the Shakespearean Romeo and Juliet story, set in the slums of New York at the coincidence of the Easter-Passover celebrations.[1] The divided factions were to have been Jews (the Capulets) and Catholics (the Montagues), thus representing a basic division in society. Even in a "musical" there was to be no evasion of the Shakespearean tragic dimension, and no more than a tenuous hopefulness in place of a happy-ever-after. For six years nothing came of the project, mostly because of Bernstein's crowded schedule as an international conductor. When in the mid-1950s Bernstein and Robbins took the matter up seriously they'd found two other collaborators: Arthur Laurents, who was to write the book, and the youthful Stephen Sondheim, who had already demonstrated remarkable talents as a lyricist. By this time the theme was slightly updated. The rival gangs were now not Jews and Catholics, but two groups of adolescents, one self-styled WASPS, the other Puerto Ricans, poverty-stricken Latin-American immigrants to the presumed White Eldorado of New York. This brought musical as well as theatrical bonuses, for New York's jazz-rock-pop culture could be enlivened by a variety of Latin-American rhythms and dance-forms.

Bernstein was fired by the audacity of the enterprise, as well he might have been, for it would be a triumph to bring off a theatre-piece that functioned within the conventions of the commercial musical while being a tragedy concerned with personal and social disintegration. Triumph he did. No one protested about the tragic dénouement, and the work's initial success in 1957 proved to be no flash in the pan. More than thirty years after the event *West Side Story* is still performed all over the world, sometimes by amateurs in performances that can barely handle the difficulties of the work, sometimes with all-star casts in elite opera houses. It was the latter high-powered presentation that was adopted by Bernstein for his "complete" recording in 1985 which, oddly enough, was the first time he had conducted the piece himself. (He had previously conducted only the so-called *Symphonic Dances*.)

Understandably, he said that he wanted at last to hear what he had written, as he had ideally conceived it. This doesn't mean that he thought such streamlined performances should become the norm, for a certain rawness and unlickedness are more appropriate to a piece about young people in the big city, waiting, nervily and twitchily, for something to happen.

The opening numbers (Nos 1–3)[2] present, in choreographed dance of dazzling éclat, the rival teenage gangs of Jets (white New Yorkers) and Sharks (coffee-coloured Puerto Ricans). In the music for both factions the mindless destructiveness of gang life is brilliantly realized balletically, the musical textures—like those of much Modern Jazz of the 1950s—being harsh and hard, with many parallel fourths and fifths and a prevalence of percussive, non-harmonic minor seconds. The tunes are fragmentary, riddled with devilish tritones, the rhythms jittery. In the Sharks' music, as compared with the Jets', a more potent hypnosis is generated by the Latin-American cross rhythms of 3/4 against 6/8. But in both musics the persistent dislocation of the accents is at once emotional and physical: this is how they walk and talk, prance and dance. Recurrently, bitonality—or rather two-part writing in which the upper part is unresolved appoggiatura to the lower—suggests their disconnectedness. The words of the "Jet Song" tell us that although the kids don't belong to society, they belong to one another, which is what gangs are about. Their couldn't-care-less defiance of the world is vividly expressed in their twittering tritones; "cool" in their heartlessness, they are savage behind the tight lips. The Puerto Rican gang music, for all its Latin exuberance, is also brittle and disorientated—in Bernstein's directive, "light and dry."

The gang-life depicted in these opening dances is public in the sense that the gangs are substitutes for society. But there are suggestions that private lives might also be feasible, for several Jets complain to their leader Riff that they suspect that Tony—co-founder with Riff of the gang—is losing enthusiasm for the cause. Riff dismisses this, on the grounds that so enterprising a youth as Tony couldn't possibly betray "the swingin'est thing," since "when you're a Jet/You're a Jet all the way." Even so, when the scene moves to a back-yard where Tony is

129

painting the sign of Doc's drugstore it seems that Tony's critics may have a case. He cannot be *merely* a Jet, for he now *works*; and the varying images of his song reflect his mixed feelings. "Something" may be coming "*cannonballing* down through the sky," but it will be "bright as a *rose*."

The action begins when we move to the Dance at the Gym (No. 4), where the Jets and Sharks meet, on what is designated as neutral ground, to decide on the next stage in their conflict. The Jet music is now a rock blues in disrupted boogie rhythm, harshly dissonant. The Sharks have a Paso Doble and a Mambo, rhythmically potent but savage. This merges into a gentler, seductively swinging Cha-cha in G major (No. 4c), traditionally a benedictory key, which here provides a transition from the public to the private life, since in the midst of the hurly-burly the Jet Tony sees the Shark Maria and falls in love "at first sight." Arbitrary and irrational barriers of race and social conditioning evaporate for the two young lovers; but Bernardo, Maria's brother, noticing the love-passage, is furious and orders Chico, whom he has brought from Puerto Rico to marry Maria, to take her home. Icily, he arranges to meet Riff, the Jet leader, at the drugstore, for a war council.

The love-motif when Tony and Maria meet consists of a rising tritone (that devilishly imperfect fifth), edging up to the perfect fifth (which in the Middle Ages used to be the musical equivalent of God!). A brief mingling of the once-rival types of dance leads into the confession of love in the famous apostrophe to *Maria*, whose Catholic name makes its point. Tony's tenor line moves in speech rhythms, trying to be articulate, in the sharp light of B major. He suspects he's found the "Something coming" that may be an answer to willfully staged destruction; and the first song-number, "Maria" (No. 5), turns the tables on the "commercial" world by being in the idiom of the pop standard as well as in the key, E flat major, most favored by standards because it lies easy for the voice. Although this is the language these young people speak (if speak they do) it is here wonderfully irradiated. The tune, flowing in triplets against the 4/4 beat, grows directly from the tritone-to-perfect-fifth motif which sounds tender yet, because of the painfully resolving dissonance, is filled with yearning. The wavering modulations, especially to mediants, also suggest something waiting to be born. We even hear the tenor's high B flat as spiritual aspiration rather than as mere exhibitionism, though that too is endemic in youth. Equilibrium between positive and negative forces becomes crucially complex in the duet "Tonight" (No. 6), which is again a corny standard in corny E flat major and in common time, yet is also an operatic ensemble powerfully, even grandly, developed. The tune itself, with its falling sixth and rising arpeggios, is continually *seeking*, abetted by its panting accompaniment and wide-ranging modulations. There's a marvelous moment when the music touches on A major, a tritone away from the initial E flat—A major being traditionally a key of youth and innocence. The number ends with a da capo of what standards call the "first eight," not in the tonic but in the softer *sub*dominant, A flat.

From this glimpse into love's private truth we return to public reality, now presented comically, if bitterly. While the boys have their war council the Puerto Rican girls, led by Anita (Bernardo's lover), sing a number about "America" (No. 7), contrasting the island of Manhattan with the Cytherean isle of Puerto Rico. Rosalia starrily presents her dream-isle pervaded by tropical breezes, pineapples and coffee-blossom; Anita punctures each verse with parody, pointing to the poverty and disease typical of the real place. The girls favor America's paradise of cars and washing machines, even though it's a sell-out to commerce and prostitution. The words are hilariously witty though their burden is sharp; and to complement them the Latin-American rhythms are compulsive but also jangled, while the modulations, if free, are incessant, flickering, directionless. Against this the Jets, led by Riff, sing their testament (No. 8) as they nervily await the arrival of the Sharks for the war council. Their number is "Cool," fragmented in rhythm yet riddled with the tritones and perfect fifths we've seen to be the heart of the love song. We don't yet grasp the meaning of this paradox, though we may sense that it suggests that the young cannot be totally irredeemable. Certainly, when Bernardo arrives to confront Riff they compromise, deciding that they won't go for an all-out rumble, but will stage a fair fight—the best man from each group to slug it out.

131

The latent possibility of love becomes patent when the scene shifts to the bridal shop where, appropriately, Maria works (Nos 8 to 9a). When Tony enters, Maria persuades him to try to stop the fight. Replacing the evil "magic" of war with the sacred power of love, they enact a mock marriage with the shop's mannequins as witnesses. This plighting of troth, obligatory for a Latin Catholic girl, is a magic moment musically, with a solemn theme undulating around repeated notes, in the mysterious flatness of G flat major (another mediant relationship). The hymn-like tune is a chorale in slow triple pulse, while chromatic intrusions poignantly hint at the death which alone can part them. This time the da capo is a tone higher, not a semitone lower as in "Tonight." The resultant key, A flat, is in both cases the same.

From this sacred moment we switch back to the perverse present: a big ensemble (No. 10) built around the "Tonight" song in its two opposed meanings: the private night of love for Tony and Maria, the public night of hatred for the gangs. William Blake said that "without Contraries [there] is no progression," a truth demonstrated in this complexly organized ensemble.[3] After savagely disparate musics in Jettish and Sharkey styles the "Tonight" tune seems to be celebrating not love but war. The panting rhythms are now angry rather than tremulous with desire, and the irony is compounded when Tony and Maria overlay the melée with their own identities, singing the tune "warmly," so that its original import soars through the ensemble's cross-grained metres. Cruder ambiguities are revealed when Anita, reaffirming the old Jacobean equation of sex and death, excitedly looks forward to sex with Bernardo, triggered by the frenzy of war—for both sides are now threatening to turn the man-to-man fight into a general "Rumble." Tony tries to persuade the contestants to call off even the "fair fight," but what was meant to be a Maria-inspired act of love perversely lets loose death. Riff assaults Bernardo and both produce knives. In the affray Bernardo stabs Riff. Tony, snatching the knife from the dying Jet, stabs Bernardo and, panic-stricken, runs off. Musically, the rumble is entirely instrumental, reaching a climax of dissonance and metrical distortion at the knifings. Hatred has triumphed over the dream of love as the wail of police-car sirens rises from the orchestral pit.

But the dream is not yet dead. Maria, ignorant of the cataclysm and double murder, sings to herself and her friends of that happy "Something coming." Her "I feel pretty" song (No. 12), performed before her mirror (a dream acted out in front of an illusion), is what the record shops call "Easy Listening" (as well as easy looking) music, being a fast Frenchified Latin-American Waltz in 3/8 and at first in E flat major, with an upward lilting and tilting phrase that follows her gestures and the inflexions of her speaking voice. Moreover, the tune moves up from E flat to F, and grows very Hispanic for a middle section in A minor and D major, wherein the voices of the other female Sharks twine with hers in parallel thirds. The da capo moves up a further tone to "blessed" G major—a sinister irony in the circumstances, for Chico, Maria's intended betrothed as distinct from her true lover, enters to tell Maria that Tony has murdered her brother, Bernardo. Chico takes a gun and leaves in pursuit of Tony; but as Maria kneels in prayer, Tony comes to her, and they reaffirm their love, which is stronger than hatred and death.

But this, it seems, can be true only in dream, for what follows is a ballet sequence which is a vision of *potential* bliss, wherein the city walls are effaced and the gangs break through into a world of space, air, and sun. The "positive" dance of the gangs is called Scherzo (No. 13c), which makes it an illusory joke; but that the dream may be more real than reality is hinted when an anonymous woman, representing humankind, carols a song about a Somewhere where there will be "a place for us,/Peace and quiet and open air," together with "time to spare,/Time to look and care" (No. 13d). The beautiful tune, with its aspiring upward sixth and drooping arpeggio, is corny only in being youthfully vulnerable; given their preconditioning, this is precisely how these young people would envisage heaven. Significantly, the key is E major, a traditionally paradisal key, being in the Baroque era the sharpest, most upward major key in common use. The tune floats, however, between E and its lower mediant C major, for consummation cannot be yet, if ever. Moreover, the C major diatonic concords are riddled with "blue notes" in *false* relation, giving the music a tenuously hopeful frailty recalling that of Copland, Bernstein's older friend and mentor. Much of Copland's music has been concerned with the rural dream of a "New Hampshire everlasting and unfallen," even in the midst of the turbulent city.

So the dream is only a dream, to be truncated by a reality as "nasty, brutish and short" as Hobbes, that seventeen-century prophet of our modern world, had said it would be. The vision fades into flashbacks of Riff and Bernardo and the knifings (No. 13e), leaving Tony and Maria once more separated by the warring sides. A still more violent return to "reality" occurs when the "real" stage replaces the visionary one, and the Jets, singly and in chorus, perform a number in "fast vaudeville style," ironically in B major (No. 14). Sondheim's wittily hilarious words debunk both the Law, in the person of Officer Krupke, and the so-called "caring professions," in the persons of psychiatrists and social workers, whom the rebel youths guy mercilessly. No one, they suggest, "wants a fella with a social disease." Although the number is grotesquely farcical, offering relief after so much accumulated tension, the point of its crass vulgarity is serious enough: only in a world where law and order and love and compassion can be so ribaldly mocked could such horrors happen. This may be why this vaudeville frolic triggers off the final catastrophe, for it leads into a duet between Maria and Anita, "A Boy Like That/I Have a Love" (No. 15), which directly confronts the fearful paradox that Tony and Maria, loving one another in the ultimate truth of love, must be divided by hate and death. We understand now why the "Tonight" love song was so ambivalent, for duality is the essence of this duet. Anita opens by singing, in "deathly" B flat minor, a lurching tune with cross accents in 3/2, alternating with 4/4. She rounds on Maria for loving "A boy like that who'd kill your brother," and advises her, since no social accommodation seems possible, to "stick to your own kind." The pungent ferocity of the song owes something to Kurt Weill, but is potent enough to serve as musical climax to the whole play. Were the music not so forceful, the effect of Maria's delayed entry would be less moving: for she, despite everything—even death—counters Anita's negation with affirmation. Her song, confessing that "I have a love, and it's all I have,/Right or wrong," does slowly triumph, the "seeking" within the song being manifest in the restless modulations, moving from blessed G major to innocent

A major, then to the sacral G flat major of the mock-marriage scene, and finally lifting again to G major. When in the coda Anita sings *Maria's* song in unison or parallel thirds with her, we recognize that this song of affirmation is a metamorphosis of "Tonight," which had always embraced "negative" tritones within its affirmation of love. Musically, the positive elements, now and at last, prove stronger than negation.

Even so, any blissful resolution is possible only *in potentia*. With extraordinary cunning and insight Bernstein ends with an inversion of values. The Jets have gathered at Doc's drugstore, where Tony is hiding in the cellar. When Anita enters with a message from Maria, the Jets taunt her in a savage dance, to parodied Sharkish music played not live, but on a juke box. It's to this mechanical music—a subtle synonym for the unreality of the so-called real or technological world—that the catastrophe occurs (No. 16), for Anita, crazed by the mob-taunting, is driven to pretend that Chico has shot Maria. Tony, overhearing, wanders into the night streets, imploring Chico to kill him too. Yet it is Maria who steps out of the darkness, to be momentarily reunited with Tony—until Chico shoots, and Tony falls. Maria catches him and he dies in her arms, to a version of the Dream Ballet music about the somewhere and somewhen in which the young may find atonement and assuagement. The funereal pulse and tolling bell (No. 17) tell us that this is a long way off. Although the key is celestial E major it again teeters to an unresolved C major, spiced with false relations—as the Dream itself had done. To tremulously unlifting, Coplandesque major seconds, we are left waiting, knowing that Americans are the last "first" people, and that they are the representatives of all humankind as they await the consummation.

A Personal Postscript

I didn't know Bernstein well, but met him on and off over the past thirty years: most recently when he was in London for a performance of his *Mass*. We had a talk—as always with him at once warm and stimulating: in the course of which he surprised me by confessing that he'd been "disappointed" that I "hadn't liked *West Side Story*." Now, I'd thought that in my book about

American music published in 1964[4] I'd been highly enthusiastic about the importance of the piece as a break-through; and in any case I wouldn't have expected so famous a man to have remembered what I'd written many years ago, nor to have cared if he had remembered. It appeared that he'd been saddened because I hadn't liked the love music as much as the hate music. Reconsidering, and having restudied words and music in depth on the occasion of the complete recording, I've come to admit that he was right, and I wrong. The love music is indeed precisely appropriate to the people who sing it and is, at the same time, miraculously re-creative. I wrote this article to make such amends as I could, and drafted a letter to Lennie to tell him what I was doing, and why. He died before I could post the letter, let alone the published article. This matters to me, if no longer to him.

NOTES

1   See Bernstein, "Excerpts from a *West Side Story* Log," *Findings* (London: Macdonald and Co., 1982), pp. 144–7.

2   The figures in brackets refer to the numbered sections in the Schirmer vocal score. These are duplicated in the 1985 Complete Recording conducted by Bernstein, and issued by Deutsche Grammophon. The order of the numbers was altered somewhat in the 1961 film, directed by Jerome Robbins and Robert Wise.

3   William Blake, "The Argument," "The Marriage of Heaven and Hell," *Complete Writings*, ed. Geoffrey Keynes (London: Oxford University Press, 1969), p. 149.

4   Wilfrid Mellers, *Music in a New Found Land* (London: Barrie and Rockliff, 1964), pp. 428–434.

10

Sondheim and the Art That Has No Name

Stephen Banfield

"Which comes first generally—the words or the music?" asks the chat-show host in Stephen Sondheim and George Furth's *Merrily We Roll Along* (1981), as they satirize the anecdotal curiosity which sustains conventional ways of talking and writing about showbiz working methods. "Generally, the contract," answers the lyricist character Charley Kringas, paraphrasing Ira Gershwin.[1] Anecdotal the curiosity may be, but at least it acknowledges different positions in which creative intercourse, so to speak, between musical theater collaborators may occur. In the worldwide spectrum of song, one might guess, words are just as likely to be added to music as vice-versa. In the Western tradition, lyric poets and theatrical lyricists from Robert Burns and Robert Louis Stevenson to W. S. Gilbert and Oscar Hammerstein have frequently worked to a "dummy" melody or, like Sondheim himself when supplying lyrics to some of Jule Styne's music in *Gypsy* (1959) and Bernstein's in *West Side Story* (1957), have fitted their words to a pre-composed tune, something to be found also in the under-valued art of opera translation.[2] Further, countless popular songs bear attributions where no attempt is made to indicate which of two or three collaborators wrote words, which composed music, bearing out Bernstein's remark about *West Side*

137

Story, that "collaboration is this great mysterious thing that gets to the point that you don't really know who wrote what."[3]

Close scrutiny of the compositional process can be fascinating and instructive, but in dealing with what (for want of a better word) is best called vernacular song, what matters is not whether words or music came first, or that they were both written by the same person, but that the relationship between them is based technically and hence aesthetically on factors quite different from the notion of "word-setting" which, with its extension "word-painting," is the only conceptual tool classical musicians are accustomed to handle. Poetry or prose "set to music" on the classical high ground is essentially appropriated and possessed by it. There is, it has been said, no marriage between words and music, only rape. The verbal text gives up its aesthetic and structural identity; it ceases to be subject to literary yardsticks. Art music's "monologic" authorial voice, like that of the camera in film, annihilates all viewpoints on the material but its own.

Michael Tippett, rallying to Suzanne Langer's powerful expression of this thesis that "music swallows words," maintains even further that this is the case not just in the realms of art music but in all song: "Once... chanting has gone over into song, then our appreciation of the words virtually ceases."[4] I believe that he is wrong and that vernacular song, especially when it aspires to the quality of wit, can be based on an interplay between verbal and musical factors giving rise to a unitary perception dependent upon them both. The art of producing this unitary perception is rarely subjected to analysis and appears to have no recognized name other than the inconveniently connotative and workaday term "songwriting." I suggest that we call it *melopoetics*. The term, or a variant of it, has already been coined by Barricelli, Scher, and others, but these and comparable writers on literature and music of their generation or an earlier one, such as Burke, Hollander, Ivey, Kramer, Myers, Smith, Stevens, Sundberg and Winn, have seldom been concerned with the vernacular matrix.[5] Hartman is something of an exception, particularly with his chapter on Joni Mitchell. Furthermore the ideas of Smith, especially on "closural allusions," and Burke, on the transformational relationships of consonants, cry out to be joined up with some of the considerations explored below.[6]

Of course, a tune can be hummed without the words and a lyric epigram enjoyed without the tune. Nevertheless, the implication of melopoetic integration is that the appearance of one without the other severely limits the degree to which the aesthetic or structural experience of the whole can be communicated. Commentators have pointed out that lyrics cannot stand in print without their tunes. For instance, John Updike acknowledges in his "Foreword" to *The Complete Lyrics of Cole Porter* that "where no tune comes to mind to fit the words, they spin themselves a bit vacuously down the page." Sondheim, too, speaking of "Oh, What a Beautiful Mornin'," has said that he "would be ashamed to put it down on paper, it would look silly ... it's a *beautiful* lyric—but not on paper." Thomas Hischak summarizes such views when he says "so many argue ... that it is a disservice to the lyricist to have his words sitting there on the page naked without benefit of the music."[7] One might compare this perception with our reaction to (non-monophonic) melody when we see it in print without its harmony, and it suggests the corollary that while lyrics are verse they are not necessarily poetry.[8] This may explain why literary critics can ignore song lyrics and "rhymes," and the lack of attention given to popular and vernacular music by many analytical and cognitive musical theorists.

However, it is worth considering *why* lyrics look odd without their music. The assumption, too often, is that as verse they are banal and empty. On occasion this may be true, but it is not the proper answer. David Lindley, a literary commentator whose passing consideration of popular lyrics is an encouraging sign, quotes the refrain of Cole Porter's "You're the Top" and lays it out on the page in the customary way:

> You're the top!
> You're the Colosseum,
> You're the top!
> You're the Louvr' Museum...[9]

And so on. This utterly misrepresents the song's underlying "quadratic" framework, the "four-beat" rhythm as it is called by

Derek Attridge, which has to take account of an extraordinarily large number of metric "silent beats," only supplied by the music.[10] Using Attridge's symbols of primary and secondary metric beats (the silent ones are in square brackets), a more representative layout shows that a great deal of the verse pattern is simply missing:

```
– – – –You're the top! – – –
[B  b]              B  [b]

– – – –You're the Colosseum,
[B  b]              B  b

– – – –You're the top! – – –
[B  b]              B  [b]

– – – –You're the Louvr' Museum;
[B  b]              B       b

– – – –You're a melody
[B  b]              B  b

From a symphony by Strauss; – – –
       B       b   B   [b]

You're a Bendel bonnet, A Shakespeare sonnet,
       B      b         B          b

You're Mickey Mouse. – – – – – – – – –
       B      b        [B          b]
```

There are almost as many silent beats as sung ones. The phenomenon is thrown into stronger relief by the more conventional ballad scansion of the verse section of the song, or at least of its first two lines:

```
At words poetic I'm so pathetic
B      b        B      b

That I always have found it best – – –
B            b         B   [b]
```

The refrain of "You're the Top" may be an extreme and sophisticated case, but theatre and other vernacular song had been progressively revelling in such metrical silences from the death of Johann Strauss the younger onwards. The reasons may have had to do with changing modes of voice production and acting (as in the *diseuse* cabaret model); but the musical point of the effect is simply that the silences allow for instrumental responses to the singer by way of "fills." This give-and-take

140

between two personae, the voice and the accompaniment, which is a function of wit (especially if improvised), comes into its own in jazz; and in a jazzy song like "You're the Top" the wit is intensified when a vocal portion of the structure shifts to unexpected positions, taking rhyme with it. Hence, "You're Mickey Mouse" triumphantly caps "Strauss" a beat early. In this instance the interplay between lines of verse and lines of music is the thing; and in vernacular song such interrelationships between the media, simultaneous and successive, are not only statutory but multi-directional. As we shall see, the words can express the music as much as the music expresses the words, and they can add layers of ambiguity to the structural progress of the whole just as harmony can add fruitful ambiguity and hence structural depth and prolongation to the progress of a melody. What we need are ways of analyzing words and music *together*, for in any good vernacular song, from nursery rhymes to the theater songs of Stephen Sondheim, the words and music enter our ear and surely structure our memory and play with our expectations in ways which we perceive as unitary. True, what we know about the hemispheres of the brain and their distinguishable functions may cause us to doubt this. Mark Booth has given this matter some consideration.[11] Yet my own brain remains stubbornly convinced of the unitary hypothesis. Redundancies and ambiguities between syllable and syllable, between note and note, and between syllable and note, on up through the levels of motif and phrase to strophe, refrain and— in the theater—the whole number, are the warp and woof of song's fabric.

Such properties may be the birthright of song, but when we begin to examine them closely it appears that they entail somewhat specialized techniques of composition and, unfortunately, concomitantly laborious techniques of analysis. Before engaging with some examples from the musical theater and, eventually, from Sondheim, it is best to establish the points at issue in a song in which, for centuries, they have been taken for granted, and in which they operate all the more effectively for that: "Baa, Baa, Black Sheep." Its initial gambit is to match a single note and its repetition with a single syllable and *its* repetition.

Example 1

Baa, baa, black sheep, have you an - y wool? Yes, sir, yes, sir, three bags full.

One for the mas - ter and one for the dame. And one for the lit - tle boy who

lives down the lane.

Given that the syllable used is an onomatopoeic exclamation, this means that until the second half-bar of the song there is an absolute unity between word and note, and the "baa" can be considered a *property* or parameter of the note, a matter of timbre, with the "b" acting in the way that a transient would help to define instrumental tone colour. Linguistic meaning does not raise its head. With the third note, musical expectations of a further repetition are thwarted, and with the change of note goes a change of syllable, still related to the initial "timbre" of a "b" and an "a", but put into a perspective of variation with the "l" of "black," rather as the tonal perspective on the first note is established by moving to the dominant. This simultaneous double change, however, is a matter of informational redundancy. In other words, we do not yet have reason to suspect that note and syllable are anything else than aspects of each other, and we may still imagine (if we are in C major) that all Cs in the piece will be voiced as "baa" and all Gs as "black." It is only with the fourth note that the web of structural meaning suddenly thickens as note and syllable first complement rather than duplicate each other. Our expectation of a repeated G to match the earlier repeated Cs is gratified, whereas an entirely new syllable, "sheep," is the unexpected "timbral" component. A clear simultaneous equation, as it were, between similarity and difference is thus first posited, further redundancy of information is avoided, and indeed the information content of the song takes a quantum leap as grammatical syntax and hence linguistic meaning appear on the scene. Only at this point do we know that we are dealing with a black sheep rather than an array of syllables beginning with "b", and that sound and sense therefore have the propensity to diverge.

It will by now be appreciated that any attempt to explain every parameter of a temporal artifact soon becomes very complicated. As an implication-realization model of musical analysis, it was developed, as is well known, by Leonard Meyer and others.[12] But as far as I am aware neither Meyer nor anyone else has employed it to deal with words as well as notes, despite the necessity of doing so if it is to stand as an explanation of how we process the totality of information aesthetically in a temporal work of art. Indeed, Meyer and Grosvenor Cooper analyzed this very tune, in its "Twinkle, Twinkle, Little Star" guise, in *The Rhythmic Structure of Music*, but again the words were not considered.[13]

Even the conventional co-ordinates of rhymes and cadences, basic matter in song, are an undeveloped object of study. Do they accomplish the same and therefore redundant thing in their respective media? We hear a rhyme, on the one hand, as same sound/different sound; and on the other, as similar sound/different sense. To a certain extent, these distinctions are simply reinforced when rhyme is accompanied by melodic cadence, as it is in basic lyrical genres like the nursery song (we actually call it "nursery rhyme"). It is easy to see that the same sound/different sound equation applies to the tune. In "Baa, Baa, Black Sheep," "wool" and "full" are sung to minims on the same beat of the bar but on different degrees of the scale. But it is less easy to find a musical equivalent for the similar sound/different sense equation, unless one begins to consider harmony as well (for instance, an interrupted cadence). For where scale degrees are concerned, sound and sense are indivisible. Intonation is a further factor which is separable in verbal rhyme but not in cadence, since its musical equivalent again seems to be the scale degree. In "Baa, Baa, Black Sheep" the contrast in verbal intonation, here nicely congruent with both syntax and sense, is between the upward, open, interrogative function of "wool" and the downward, affirmative closure of "full," reflecting the very meaning of the word itself, since with it both the poetic line and the question-and-answer discourse themselves become "full." Yet while rhyme may flourish without these multiple concordances, in music it all comes down to the one distinction between the dominant scale degree ($\hat{5}$) at the end of the first line and the tonic closure ($\hat{1}$) at the end of the second. Try singing "full" to any other scale degree and the point is appreciated. Harmony, on the other hand, offers musical cadence the structural subtleties of simultaneous sound unavailable to the single-note progression of rhyme.

Added to these multiple co-ordinates in "Baa, Baa, Black Sheep," the ways in which the words and the notes keep converging (as in the parallels of repeated notes and verbal phrases in "Yes, sir, yes, sir" and "One for the ...") are more than enough to tell our ears to hear the song as a single aesthetic entity in which the strategies of similarity and difference, of repetition and contrast, in syllable and note are mutually illuminating. This is not to say that different words cannot be set with equally good effect to the same tune. Any strophic song aims to do this in successive stanzas; and "Ah Vous Dirai-je, Maman," the *alter ego* (and probable source) of "Baa, Baa, Black Sheep," furnishes a comparable phenomenon. The point, of course, is that each song or stanza requires a variant analysis. However, applying the considerations detailed here, it is difficult not to view the word/music integration of "Baa, Baa, Black Sheep" as an enrichment of the original, for its extra notes and syllables in the first line and greater grammatical density are an artful elaboration of the French song's simple prosody. "Twinkle, Twinkle, Little Star" is an intriguingly different melopoetic match again, broader from the start in that the initial "unit" is a two-note figure and a two-syllable word, and developed over five stanzas.

Exhausting and even banal though such analysis may appear, there is no way of avoiding it if we really want to assess a vernacular songwriter's craft. To take the interplay of rhyme and melody a stage further, let us consider "Bill," with music by Jerome Kern and lyrics by P. G. Wodehouse, written for and then cut from the 1918 show *Oh Lady! Lady!!* and eventually heard in *Show Boat* (1927), perhaps with revisions by Oscar Hammerstein II.[14]

In the refrain, a straightforward rhyme (face/grace; components of a list and hence the same part of speech) is matched

Example 2

equally straightforwardly with melodic sequence. The next rhyme, however, introduces a high level of ambiguity. Suddenly the verbal syntax broadens, and instead of a rhyme coming as a "masculine" one on the corresponding fourth syllable ("kind"), it proves to be a "feminine" one on the two following syllables ("that you"), the first a connective, the second a pronoun, while the expected rhyme, "find," is hidden away as an internal one. The incongruity of rhyming these blatantly non-substantive elements of the syntax with a two-syllable noun, "statue," contributes a degree of wit—we hear the feminine weak syllable (you/-ue) as though it were a pun. What is crucial, however, is the manner in which the ambiguity is multiplied by the music. First, the syncopation undermines the beat and creates ambiguity as to whether the last three notes in the top system's melody are still part of the three-note stepwise motif bracketed in the accompaniment. Then, more tellingly, the ambiguity is intensified in the next bar by fracturing of the sequence, for the stepwise fall begins a tone lower than it should on the word "statue." At the same time, it appears to reinstate the rhythm of

145

the motif, only to reconstrue it as four quavers connecting back to the beginning of the refrain's tune. Meanwhile, the words short-circuit the massive expansion of information-content by actually describing the rich structural confusion we are left with at this point: "And I can't explain." Moreover, the accompaniment also contributes richly to the *locus* with its own uses of the three-note motif. As bracketed in example 2, we hear the third term in the series of the initial rising melodic sequence arriving correctly, a step higher (starting on G), but incorrectly, a beat late, at the first point of verbal ambiguity. The fourth term echoes this in the following bar (system 2, bar 1) by starting on the second beat, but in the bass register and having missed a step (starting on B flat, not A), and only to prove an anticipation, in canon at a beat's distance, of the fractured sequence of the upper part. Of course, how much of this is heard depends on how the song is performed and on the effect of Robert Russell Bennett's orchestration, or whatever is substituted for it. But it is fair to say that the nuances described above, as well as the reflexive colloquialism of "And I can't explain," are not so much a textual imperative which must not be lost as an invitation to performer-freedom by which they will stand to gain. Further, as noted earlier with "Baa, Baa, Black Sheep" and "Twinkle, Twinkle, Little Star," different words to the same tune will once again enrich the scope of analysis rather than undermine it. The second strophe of "Bill" shifts the ambiguities around somewhat at the points discussed above. For instance, "comfy and roomy" resolves what in the first strophe we construed as melodic ambiguity, while "Feels natural to me" enhances the self-explanatory properties of the verbal text.

Anyone who knows Sondheim's work will not be surprised to find him revelling in such techniques as we have been examining, and his aesthetic as a writer of songs for the theatre is articulated by countless examples. For instance, as I have attempted to demonstrate elsewhere, the melopoetic synaesthesia implicit at the beginning of "Baa, Baa, Black Sheep" is spectacularly worked out on both the smallest and largest levels and extended to other parameters in *Sunday in the Park with George* (1984). On the smallest level, as with "Baa, Baa, Black Sheep," onomatopoeia is again the agent, when in the

song "The Day Óff" the artist Georges Seurat imagines monologues for the two dogs he is painting and includes their barks,
but in this case the continuum is developed much farther, from
word and note through chord and harmonic sonority. Parallels
might be drawn, for instance, with avant-garde morphology in
Berio and Joyce.[15]

Time and again Sondheim shows this kind of awareness of
the smallest cells out of which music and text are formed, the
unitary signals of communication that know of no distinction
between the media of music and language *before* those signals
combine to form messages. Treating it like a chord or a note, he
will often itemize a syllable (or pair of syllables) as an onomatopoeic identity, as an exclamation (or humming syllable) or
even as a spoken letter. "Yoo-hoo," for example, is a favourite
morpheme (influenced, perhaps, by its appearance in Cole
Porter's Song, "After You"), presumably both because it is in
itself a microcosm. of melopoetic generation (it is a rhyme)
while still remaining impossible to make *sense* of without its
sound as a kind of musical call. It affords the title of two different songs, one cut from *Sunday in the Park with George*, the
other to be found in his early musical *Climb High* (1950–1952).
It also occurs, as a kind of miniature refrain, in "By the Sea"
from *Sweeney Todd* (1979) where it appears as an articulated
melisma of the word "you" and is immediately repeated as Mrs.
Lovett's promenade greeting, transformed from a seagull call,
"Hoo! Hoo!" Japanese melopoetic transformations of these two
usages occur in *Pacific Overtures* (1976). "Yo-ho!" is used as a
recurrent, chanted signal of recognition in "Welcome to
Kanagawa," and in "Four Black Dragons" "Hai! Hai!" represents
not seagulls but "women ... screaming like gulls," where, as
with the dog barks in "The Day Off" and in accordance with
Japanese theatrical conventions, "instrumental" imitations
(handclaps) are involved as well, a synaesthetic gesture which
reminds us that the Western "Yoo-hoo" greeting is similarly
synaesthetic, being more or less unimaginable without a wave.
Sondheim is not alone, of course, in the use of spelled-out
letters. The Gershwins' song "Do, Do, Do" from *Oh, Kay!* (1926),
and indeed the show's title, offer earlier examples of the same
mentality, "Do, Do, Do" being a brilliant example of witty con-

struction and transformation using such building blocks, as the tiniest extract will suggest.[16]

Example 3

[Moderato grazioso]

Ba - by, see, It's A. B. C.

Here the technique lies not just in the trisyllabic rhyming but in the fact that the melody notes suggest a permutating series (D, C, B flat, becoming D, B flat, C) at the point where the alphabetical series "A. B. C." is spoken. The reciprocity of permutation is immediately clinched by the next line (with its melodic sequence), "I love you and you love me." Compare Sondheim's use of permutation and reciprocity in the "I-O-U" passage (to Jule Styne's music) in "Together Wherever We Go" from *Gypsy* (1959), where the virtuosic material of the rhymes is eventually reduced to vowels, even more elemental than letters, to the point where he appears to be able to keep just three of them in permutation, indefinitely spinning out linguistic meaning (we hear "I-O-U-I-O-U-O"). Not that the melody permutates three notes at this point; but its methodically falling contours do begin to rise again, to a question rather than exclamations, just as the vowel sequence might begin to suggest a palindrome.[17]

Example 4

[Moderately]

ROSE: HERBIE: A du - o!
What - ev - er the boat____ I row. you row.____ What - ev - er the row

LOUISE: A tri - o! HERBIE: Who.
____ I hoe. you hoe.____ And an - y I - O - U I owe. you owe.

me? Oh, no, you owe! ALL:
No. we owe. To - geth - er!

Sooner or later, however, such synaesthetic signals and universal connections springing from the single gesture do have to combine to form messages in separable media. What happens when we take on the regular note-to-note and syllable-to-syllable *procedure* of songs? Can the two media really hope to structure time with one accord? Perhaps a genuinely unitary melopoesis is an ideal rather than an ever-present deep structure even in the meticulous and highly self-conscious work of Sondheim, but we may nonetheless benefit from considering three ways in which he approaches it.

The first is through the kind of structural wit, the exploitation of ambiguity, that we considered in "Bill." Here the search must be for processes of expansion which are not quite identical in the words and the music, not quite congruent, but with a control of tension between the two and an establishment of structural proposition unitary and tight enough to furnish one *meaning* for the song in both media while giving rise to *ambiguities* between them. This is the real test of interdependence, of the quality of wit in a song. Elsewhere I have analyzed the song "I'm Calm" from *A Funny Thing Happened on the Way to the Forum* (1962), a slight number but a particularly clear example of melopoetic structuring, in order to demonstrate, in a way that perhaps can only be done with the aid of graphic representation, what is at stake and what is possible.[18] Here a less exhaustive example can be given and some of the same conclusions reached, by using the song "Lovely," again from *A Funny Thing Happened on the Way to the Forum*.[19]

Example 5

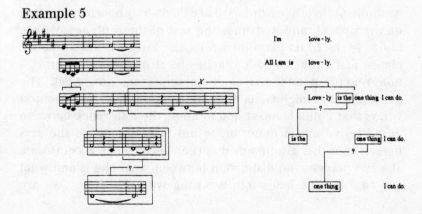

149

It is apparent that Sondheim was self-consciously honing his technique on this score. As in "I'm Calm," the basic constructional cell that opens the song proper (after initial underscoring and a preparatory accompaniment figure) is very simple: an upbeat crotchet antecedent on the subdominant scale degree ($\hat{4}$) moving by conjunct voice-leading to a repeated-minim downbeat consequent on the dominant ($\hat{5}$) (example 5 gives the first eight-bar phrase). All the terms involved in this description denote something subsidiary leading to something primary, and this is not only what the initial words "I'm lovely" replicate in their subject-predicate construction (for the adjective is the point and indeed the title of the song); but it is what they gloss and strengthen in the next line ("All I am is lovely"), just as the four quavers in the melody simultaneously gloss the crotchet E when the musical phrase is repeated. So far, therefore, verbal and musical meanings reinforce each other without ambiguity; but they do so only long enough to establish their mutuality. To continue the parallelism beyond the second phrase would be, rather as with a melodic sequence that continues too long, to court redundancy of information (which is to say that the third term in a series confirms meaning). Instead, Sondheim springs a surprise by creating different distributional paths for music and words at the third repetition (compare the vertical alignments of melody and lyrics in example 5). The melody retains the same cyclic pattern, further (but only slightly) varying the four-quaver upbeat figure, while the lyrics suddenly adopt a grammatical phase-shift, "lovely" moving from complement to subject (X in example 5). In other words, we are thrown by hearing the word on the upbeat, and it stymies the rest of the sentence, which, not to speak of its plain incorrectness, tails off into a relative clause just as the melody reaches its strongest point through note-repetition and arrival at an important downbeat. The point of this ambiguity, its dramatic as opposed to its structural wit, is that Philia is too stupid to know the difference between an adjective and a noun; or, to put it another way, she gets herself into this grammatical corner because, as a courtesan, she can perceive no distinction between what she is and what she can do. She leads into the song with the lines: "We are taught beauty and grace, and no more. I cannot add, or spell, or anything. I have but one talent." Years later another of Sondheim's characters, Georges Seurat, will voice a similar perception ("I am what I do"), but in "Lovely" the intention is comic. Ironically, though, later in the song Philia shows rather more command of syntax than one would expect when she avows, with meticulous grammar, "I can neither sew,/Nor cook, nor read or write my name." Sondheim later thought better of it; in subsequent printings of the lyrics, and on the film sound-track, he changed "or" to another "nor," which is however less convenient to sing.

The X ambiguity between words and melody is the main one, but there are subsidiary ambiguities at this point within each medium (see the boxed alternatives of distributional meaning in example 5). Philia's third line is such a solecism that we tend to discount the vestiges of parallel construction, but they are there. The verb "is" still occurs on the pivoting quavers (though now on the third rather than the fourth), and this apprehension of paral-lelism may lead to another, that "one thing" is equivalent to "lovely" in assonance. In the music, on the other hand, the ambiguous readings concern precisely the point at which the ambiguity of lyric construction has been resolved into the lame-ness of "I can do." The crotchet rest (surely the indication that Philia recognizes she is about to utter a howler) disguises the pos-sible "meaning" of two more minims (this meaning is confirmed eight bars later), while the length of the last note of the phrase may suggest a parallel with the original F sharps, an arrival point of the mediant ($\hat{3}$) as complement to the earlier dominant, both preceded by a crotchet a step lower (not tabulated in example 5). This last connection is as musically unremarkable as its verbal counterpart—the anticlimactic "do" referring back to "lovely"—is ludicrous, and the incongruity seals the wit.

This essay does not have the space and, I suspect, the reader does not have the patience to allow this degree of explanation for the whole song. However, I should like to mention some salient points and levels at which redundancy of information between words and music is avoided and ambiguities are creatively courted. In the song's second eight-bar phrase the displacement of "lovely" is not paralleled, but neither is the substitute word ("winsome") retained for all three pairs of F sharp minims. A punning rhyme ("in some," recalling Wodehouse's "that you/statue" in "Bill") gives us something to smile at instead. Then the long note which end-stopped the first phrase (on the word "do") receives attention. Its complement, up an octave, rhymes ("true"), but while the same note is then used again as a fulcrum into the release or "middle eight" of the melody, thereby incidentally confirming the congruence of meaning between these long notes and repeated minims, its word ("Oh") now pulls in the opposite direction, away from identity, not just by failing to rhyme with its antecedent (it proves to be, instead, itself the antecedent of the later rhyme "sew"), but also by being merely an exclamation, not part of a grammatical phrase. Most notable, perhaps, is the way in which at the point where everything might be expected to tie back in, namely the return of the A section of the melody, Sondheim completely breaks the pattern by using the word "happy" instead of returning to "lovely." It rhymes with nothing and, more important and most typically for him, puts a doubly broad interpretation upon the phrase structure because of its verbal meaning, which is not as it first appears ("I'm happy") but (to paraphrase) "I'm content simply to be lovely." In fact the phrase structure then doubles again to encompass the last four bars as well, by the use of the subordinate conjunction "for." Other points to note in these last four bars are reminiscences of earlier ambiguities. "Merely" reflects the rogue placing of "lovely" discussed above and, close on its heels, the corollary "one thing" recurs. The melody of the entire stanza is given in example 6.[20]

Before leaving "Lovely" it is well worth seeing what Sondheim does with his strophe after its first statement. The second stanza is sung by Hero, who makes a number of minute changes of melopoetic interpretation. For the first time we are invited to consider three repeated minims as a musical unit (see the third system of example 5) because the word "lovely" is extended to become "loveliness." Then, to use Benedict Nightingale's phrase about Sondheim's *Into the Woods* (1987), "happy" avoids being predictable in its unpredictability, for this time around it does show syntactical self-sufficiency before reverting to its earlier, dependent sense ("And I'm happy, /Happy that I'm lovely").[21] Most ingeniously, "one thing" now

Example 6

articulates an even further broadening of the strophe's culmination. Instead of referring back to "being lovely"—"*it's* one
thing"—it now refers forward: "*there's* one thing," a thing which
then has to be identified, neatly furnishing the occasion for a
final four-bar phrase extension to climax the song melodically
in the form of a *petite reprise*, while the lyrics manage to weave
in both the earlier "loveliness" and Philia's "can do," though
this occasions a return of grammatical solecism, now on Hero's
lips as well as Philia's since by this time they are singing
together. Loveliness, for all it can do, cannot *do* a gift.[22]

Example 7

However, the ultimate ambiguity of "lovely" is at the dramatic level, a larger level than I have hitherto charted, one at which meaning changes although both words and music are unambiguously repeated. This first occurs between stanzas 1 and 2 of the song, since Hero by and large repeats Philia's words but transforms them from a first-person apology or rote-lesson (she has, after all, been *taught* that she is lovely) into an ecstatic, apostrophic paean of love—though Philia's matter-of-fact acceptance of the adulation, when she echoes Hero's "some dream come true" with her "True," comically undercuts it and creates a further ambiguity. But of course the culmination of the song's ambiguities occurs when Pseudolus reprises it, with virtually the same love-song lyrics, to the dragged-up Hysterium. This time the apostrophe does come first. Hysterium needs it, as flattery, in order to be persuaded that he is convincing as a woman. However, Pseudolus cannot resist the odd verbal ambiguity of his own ("frighteningly lovely") within this shared dramatic one.

One of the conclusions to be drawn from such analyses may seem a curious one. It can be sensed in "Bill," with its homely half-sentimental humor in the idea of his "comfy and roomy" knee to compensate for lack of looks and brain. It is that, while it is the business of music to create ambiguities as a matter of serious taste (we do not normally expect to laugh at a sequence or interrupted cadence), the business of lyrics is to create wit by similar means. There is a delicious example of this in "Could I Leave You," from *Follies*. We appreciate the ambiguity, in the sense of the three-step extension and reinterpretation of the meaning of the title-word "leave," at the lines:

Could I leave you?
No, the point is,
Could you leave me?
Well, I guess you could leave me the house

and "the Braques and Chagalls," and so on.[23] We also appreciate the step-by-step transformation of meaning of the two-note motif that conveys it musically, from a rising 2nd through its extended inversion (two falling 2nds making a 3rd) to a further intervallic increase (falling 4th) then lowered further by a sequence. Yet we call one lyric wit and the other musical seriousness. In the end, though, the difference between smiling outwardly at witty words or inwardly at good melodic practice may be immaterial. Particularly where the whole structural accomplishment of a song is concerned, the sense of overall triumphant enjoyment can make nonsense of the distinction, for it is not one which our applauding hands recognize.

This brings me to the second consideration, which has indeed been implicit throughout my discussion of "Lovely": the use of a title to govern the melopoetic structure of a whole song. There is not space here to demonstrate it fully, but pointers can be offered. The title is an aspect of a vernacular song's structure which has been ignored by academic analysts because it is simply not a consideration in most classical music and lyric poetry. Yet here, above all, is the need for a phrase which is memorable because it fuses words and music into a single, more or less detachable unit of perception. We might almost call it a "jingle," for the same requirement applies in musical advertising, if only for the practical reason that a prospective purchaser must remember what the product is called or be able to hum it in the shop. How and where this unit is embedded in the song will vary, as will the scope of any larger unit of which it may form part and thereby act as a kind of emblem. Either or both may be at the beginning, at a later point of arrival, or at the end, and may be led up to or led away from or both—hence the various terms "motif," "hook," "tag," "chorus," "refrain," "release," one often nested within another. The context will normally be colloquial. Verbally it may involve anything from a single word or monosyllabic exclamation to a metaphor, proverb or epigram. Musically it may range from a single chord or harmonic progression or tiny melodic motif to a complete quadratic section of tune with cadence or even tonic closure. Again, one may "remember" one within the other, even across the two media. The melody of "Smoke Gets in Your Eyes," for instance, tends to be recalled from the front end, as it were, whereas the verbal title phrase attaches to a later peregrination. The procedure may be studiedly casual, as in "Smoke Gets in Your Eyes," or self-consciously witty or rhetorical, as with many of Sondheim's songs.

155

Sondheim tends to build songs either from an initial melopoetic cell, as we saw with "Lovely," or towards a melopoetic point
of arrival. One might call the first type "motif" songs, the second
"refrain" songs. Once such *loci* have been identified, one of the
primary issues is whether or not our listening and understanding are structured around and between them in verbal
and musical terms that are both congruent and interdependent.
The song "Free," once again from *A Funny Thing Happened on
the Way to the Forum*, furnishes an elementary example.[24] Here
the one overwhelming idea which justifies the song's existence
is the slave Pseudolus's desire to be free; and it is accomplished
in one note and one syllable. One might object to calling this
either a motif or a refrain. It is nonetheless functionally impec-
cable, and Pseudolus's antecedents always lead to his master
Hero's consequents. This integration of the dramatic structure
as well is also typical of Sondheim's striving for the mutual rein-
forcement, or witty contradiction, of parameters, almost like a
kind of integral serialism. The slave leads, the master follows,
though only he can authorize the vital act of freedom. Thus
Pseudolus leads the melody first to a cadence on the dominant
note B, which nonetheless has to be supplied by Hero after
Pseudolus has deflected it down the octave as well as down to A
sharp.

Example 8

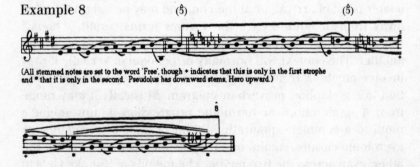

(All stemmed notes are set to the word 'Free', though + indicates that this is only in the first strophe
and * that it is only in the second. Pseudolus has downward stems, Hero upward.)

But the real goal for the word must be the upper tonic (a sort
of symbolization of the exclamation mark), eventually reached
with a fair amount of Beethovenian repetition and cadential
augmentation, the verbal equivalent of which is Pseudolus's
insistence that Hero spell it out "the long way." Here the note

shares meaning on the level of the letter, not just the word or syllable. Perhaps Sondheim had the psychological programme of Beethoven's Fifth Symphony, its concern with destiny and liberty, somewhere at the back of his mind. This upper tonic goal is reached through Pseudolus's climbing scale figures, modulating with the help of the A sharp's enharmonic reinterpretation, but Pseudolus himself only anticipates the note (and the word) in passing. Again, it is Hero who caps it, literally, if we use the graphic notation which, I hope, clarifies the discussion in example 8.

This deals with the chorus, and its antecedent-consequent structure is mirrored in macrocosm when we note that in the verse the word "free" is led up to repeatedly but never sung. Thus, to identify another point, the verse mediates between dialogue and song, for although Hero speaks the word its melodic and rhythmic clothing are not yet supplied.

Less ambitious title techniques are easily brought to mind from *West Side Story*. "Tonight," "Maria," "Cool," and "America" are all examples of how to structure a song logically from a single word. "Tonight" begins, after its verse, with a bisyllabic verbal motif (the title word) in conjunction with a two-note musical one. Both are immediately repeated, the word exactly, the musical motif with different pitches and intervallic shape but the same rhythm and metric placement. Our brain asks two questions simultaneously: "What about tonight?" and "What are these two-times-two-equals-four notes?" Back comes the simultaneous answer, glossing, expanding and explaining the connections between the notes and elaborating on the word. The downward 2nd is repeated a 5th higher so as to lead both pentatonically into itself and into the first note of the upward 4th. Verbally, it explains that "it all began tonight." More crucially, the two media do not merely explain themselves simultaneously, the explain each other. We hear, at least subtextually, the words saying to us "it all began [with the musical motif we have called] 'Tonight'." At the same time the six-note musical gloss on the first four notes says, as it were, "this song is going on about the word 'Tonight'; it's (as Ira Gershwin put it in a different context) 'blah blah blah blah tonight'."[25]

This leads me to my third and final consideration, again

hinted at in "Bill": the use of reflexivity within the media, as when the words *actually describe what the structure of the music is doing*. Perhaps this is a natural destination for a creative mind as self-consciously integral as Sondheim's. Is he conscious that this may be a way of disarming the final barrier between words and music by countering the inescapable fact that, in addition to their formal structure, words (*pace* the critical forces of deconstructionism) are actually *about* something other than themselves, for they convey discursive meanings in the theater in a way not open to music, which can ultimately only be about itself? Whatever the answer, making the words describe the musical process by which they are simultaneously conveyed is a surprisingly simple and frequent gambit. Sometimes it is done within a general context of verbal abstraction; at other times one becomes aware of it by adding a level of meaning to the external one. The last word of the song "Good Thing Going" from *Merrily We Roll Along*, for instance, is "gone." The last word of "Poems" from *Pacific Overtures* is "End." "Good Thing Going" starts with the phrase "It started out like a song"; indeed, the "good thing" can on one level be taken to be the song itself. Perhaps the most audacious example is in "Not a Day Goes By" from *Merrily We Roll Along*, in which a heart-stoppingly beautiful, slowly-spun melodic and harmonic sequence is accompanied by the words, ostensibly describing a friendship:

> I keep thinking, when does it end?
> That it can't get much better much longer.
> But it only gets better and stronger,
> And deeper and nearer...[26]

Suddenly realising that the song is talking about itself can be the greatest shock of all along the road of melopoetic awareness; but the reflexive dimension of song is properly another subject for another occasion.

NOTES
1 Stephen Sondheim and George Furth, *Merrily We Roll Along* (Music Theatre International, 1982), I-4–29. Ira Gershwin, *Lyrics On Several Occasions* (1959; rpt. London: Omnibus Press, 1978), p. 42. Portions of this chapter are based on material

from my book, *Sondheim's Broadway Musicals* (1993). I am grateful to the University of Michigan Press for permission to use this material.

2 See V. C. Clinton-Baddeley, *Words for Music* (Cambridge: Cambridge University Press, 1941), pp. 92–9; Percy M. Young, *Sir Arthur Sullivan* (London: J. M. Dent & Sons, 1971), p. 171; Arthur Jacobs, *Arthur Sullivan: A Victorian Musician* (Oxford: Oxford University Press, 1984), p. 273; Hugh Fordin, *Getting to Know Him: Oscar Hammerstein II: A Biography* (New York: Random House, 1977), p. 191; and Robert Louis Stevenson, "Songs of Travel" (in *Poems* [London: Chatto & Windus, 1910]), of which "The Vagabond" and "Whither Must I Wander?" are respectively subtitled "To an Air of Schubert" and "To the tune of Wandering Willie."

3 Craig Zadan, *Sondheim & Co.* (2nd ed., New York: Harper & Row, 1989), p. 25.

4 Suzanne Langer, "The Principle of Assimilation," *Feeling and Form* (London: Routledge & Kegan Paul, 1953), p. 152. Michael Tippett, "Conclusion," *A History of Song*, ed. Denis Stevens (London: Hutchinson, 1960), p. 462.

5 Jean-Pierre Barricelli, *Melopoiesis: Approaches to the Study of Literature and Music* (New York: New York University Press, 1988). *Music and Text: Critical Enquiries*, edited by Steven Paul Scher (Cambridge: Cambridge University Press, 1992). Kenneth Burke, "On Musicality in Verse," *The Philosophy of Literary Form* (1941; rpt. Berkeley: University of California Press, 1973), pp. 369–78. John Hollander, *Vision and Resonance: Two Senses of Poetic Form* (New York: Oxford University Press, 1975). Donald Ivey, *Song: Anatomy, Imagery, and Styles* (New York: Schirmer Books,1970). Lawrence Kramer, *Music and Poetry: The Nineteenth Century and After* (Berkeley: University of California Press, 1984). Peter Myers, *The Sound of Finnegans Wake* (New York: Macmillan, 1992). Barbara Herrnstein Smith, *Poetic Closure: A Study of How Poems End* (Chicago: University of Chicago Press, 1968). John Stevens, *Words and Music in the Middle Ages: Song, Narrative, Dance and Drama, 1050–1350* (Cambridge: Cambridge University Press, 1986). Johan Sundberg, Lennart Nord and Rolf Carlson, *Music, Language, Speech and Brain* (New York: Macmillan, 1991). James Anderson Winn, *Unsuspected Eloquence: A History of the Relations between Poetry and Music* (New Haven, CT: Yale University Press, 1981).

6 Charles O. Hartman, "Joni Mitchell: To Whom It May Concern," *Jazz Text: Voice and Improvisation in Poetry, Jazz, and Song* (Princeton, NJ: Princeton University Press, 1991), pp. 96–120. Smith, *Poetic Closure*, pp. 172–82.

7 John Updike, "Foreword," *The Complete Lyrics of Cole Porter*, ed. Robert Kimball (London: Hamish Hamilton, 1983), p. xii. Stephen Sondheim, "Theater Lyrics," *Playwrights, Lyricists, Composers on Theater*, ed. Otis L. Guernsey (New York: Dodd, Mead, 1974), p. 64. Thomas S. Hischak, *Word Crazy: Broadway Lyricists from Cohan to Sondheim* (New York: Praeger, 1991), p. xiv.

8 See, however, *The Poetry of Song: Five Tributes to Stephen Sondheim*, ed., George Robert Minkoff and J.D. McClatchy (New York: Poetry Society of America, 1992). Here an eloquent case is made for treating Sondheim's lyrics as poetry, comparable with that of Emily Dickinson and others.

9 David Lindley, *Lyric* (London: Methuen, 1985), pp. 33–4.

10 Derek Attridge, *The Rhythms of English Poetry* (London: Longman, 1982), passim. For an approach to the problem from the opposite end – the compression of poetic feet into quadratic beats – see Ann Clark Fehn and Rufus Hallmark, "Text and Music in Schubert's Pentameter *Lieder*: A Consideration of Declamation," *Studies in the History of Music*, vol. 1: *Music and Language* (New York: Broude Brothers, 1983), pp. 204–46.

11 Mark W. Booth, *The Experience of Songs* (New Haven, CT: Yale University Press, 1981), pp. 65–70. See also Claire Gérard & Catherine Auxiette, "The Role of Melodic and Verbal Organization in the Reproduction of Rhythmic Groups by Children," *Music Perception* vi/2 (1988), pp. 173–92, in which the authors' experiments suggest that the reciprocal memory coding of words and melody to rhythm may be different for musical and non-musical children. This article is representative of potential illumination from a neighbouring discipline of which it has scarcely been possible to take account here.

12 See Leonard B. Meyer, *Emotion and Meaning in Music* (Chicago: University of Chicago Press, 1956); *Music, the Arts and Ideas: Patterns and Predictions in Twentieth-century*

Culture (Chicago: University of Chicago Press, 1967); *Explaining Music: Essays and Explorations* (Berkeley: University of California Press, 1973); and the critique of his work by Jonathan Dunsby and Arnold Whittall in *Music Analysis in Theory and Practice* (London: Faber & Faber, 1988).

13 Grosvenor W. Cooper and Leonard B. Meyer, *The Rhythmic Structure of Music* (Chicago: University of Chicago Press, 1960), pp. 12–23.

14 *Show Boat*, vocal score (London: Wise Publications, 1990), pp. 203–5.

15 Stephen Sondheim, *Sunday in the Park with George* ([New York]: Revelation Music Publishing Corp. & Rilting Music, Inc., 1987), pp. 59–66. For further discussion see Banfield, *Sondheim's Broadway Musicals*, pp. 370–73.

16 Stephen Sondheim, *Sweeney Todd: The Demon Barber of Fleet Street*, vocal score ([New York]: Revelation Music Publishing Corp. & Rilting Music, Inc., 1987), pp. 64–76. Stephen Sondheim, *Pacific Overtures*, vocal score ([New York]: Revelation Music Publishing Corp. & Rilting Music, Inc., 1977), pp. 38–52, 87–105. "Do, Do, Do," *Gershwin On Broadway (from 1919 to 1933)*, (n. p.: Warner Bros. Publications Inc, 1987), pp. 201–4. For a discussion of Porter's "After You" and its melopoetics, see Allen Forte, *The American Popular Ballad of the Golden Era: 1924–1950* (Princeton, N.J.: Princeton University Press, 1995), pp. 118–23. Forte actually gives Porter's song title as "After You, Who".

17 Jule Styne and Stephen Sondheim, "Together Wherever We Go," *Gypsy*, vocal score (n.p.: Chappell Music Co., 1960), pp. 133–43.

18 See Banfield, *Sondheim's Broadway Musicals*, pp. 106–12.

19 Sondheim, "Lovely," *A Funny Thing Happened on the Way to the Forum*, vocal score (n. p.: Chappell Music Co., 1964), pp. 55–60, 130–4.

20 *Ibid.*

21 Benedict Nightingale, first-night review of the London production of *Into the Woods*, the (London) *Times*, 22 September 1990, p. 22.

22 Sondheim, "Lovely," *A Funny Thing Happened on the Way to the Forum*, vocal score (n. p.: Chappell Music Co., 1964), pp. 55–60, 130–4.

23 Sondheim, "Could I Leave You," *Follies*, ([New York]: Range Road Music Inc., Quartet Music Inc., Rilting Music Inc., and Burthen Music Co. Inc., 1971), pp. 171–81.

24 "Free," *A Funny Thing Happened on the Way to the Forum*, vocal score, pp. 35–44.

25 Leonard Bernstein and Stephen Sondheim, "Balcony Scene," *West Side Story*, vocal score (London: Chappell, 1959), pp. 63–71. Gershwin, "Blah, Blah Blah," *Lyrics On Several Occasions*, p. 151.

26 Sondheim, "Poems," *Pacific Overtures*, vocal score ([New York]: Revelation Music Publishing Corp & Rilting Music Inc., 1984), pp. 76–86. Sondheim, "Good Thing Going" and "Not a Day Goes By," *Merrily We Roll Along*, vocal score, pp. 164–8, 193–7.

Index